Personal and Social Development *for All*

Colleen McLaughlin
and Richard Byers

David Fulton Publishers
London

David Fulton Publishers Ltd
Ormond House, 26–27 Boswell Street, London WC1N 3JZ

www.fultonpublishers.co.uk

First published in Great Britain by David Fulton Publishers 2001

Note: The right of Colleen McLaughlin and Richard Byers to be identified as the authors of this work has been asserted by them in accordance with the Copyright, Designs and Patents Act 1988.

Copyright © Colleen McLaughlin and Richard Byers 2001

British Library Cataloguing in Publication Data
A catalogue record for this book is available from the British Library.

ISBN 1–85346–643–3

Typeset by Book Production Services, London
Printed in Great Britain by Bell & Bain Ltd, Glasgow

Contents

Acknowledgements

We wish to acknowledge the contributions of the following people who supported us in planning and compiling this book, either by participating in focus group discussions or by sharing materials and ideas with us:

- Dorothy Ainsley, Elmbrook School, Basildon
- Ron Babbage, St. Johns School, Bedford
- Oliver Caviglioli, Woodlands School, Chelmsford
- Clare Dunleavy, Red Gates School, New Malden
- Suzanne Farrell, Rutland House School, Nottingham
- Linda Ferguson, Clayton School, Peterborough
- Will Fletcher, Watling View School, St Albans
- Phil Goss, Ickburgh School, Hackney
- Tina Harvey, St. Anns School, Morden
- Mark Houlton, Littleton House School, Cambridge
- Mike Jelly, Edith Borthwick School, Braintree
- Hazel Lawson, Greenside School, Stevenage
- Dave Mitchelmore, Watergate School, Lewisham
- Peter McPartland, Trinity School, Dagenham
- James Pester, The Ryes School, Sudbury
- Joe Standen, John F. Kennedy School, Newham
- David Victor, Lancaster School, Southend

We would like to thank Julie Cutter and Peggy Nunn for their invaluable help and endless patience in the final production of the manuscript. We are, as ever, so grateful.

Introduction

> The centre of education is the individual. If we are to achieve a genuinely human education we must return again to the person before us, the child, the adolescent, the adult, the individual who is ready, however dimly and in need of however much support, to adventure both further out into his experience and further in to it; who is ready in some part of himself, to risk himself in order to become more than he now is. The teacher, the tutor, can provide conditions and the support for such a journey – but the journey itself can only be made by the assenting and autonomous individual.
>
> (Abbs 1974)

The emphasis on the person and the human processes of education in this quotation from Abbs is one that we would support. Education is above all a human process and one in which we are learning all the time from our actions and environments. This truism needs restating, for many would argue that recent educational policy in England and Wales has emphasised the instrumental and mechanistic. Personal and social education is back on the curriculum policy agenda and we welcome that. We have not entitled this book 'personal and social education for all', though, because we aim to take a wider view than the curricular one.

The two assumptions underlying this work are that teachers contribute to personal and social development in many contexts – in the climate of the school, in their interpersonal interactions, in the planned curriculum and in other routines and procedures that exist. The other assumption is that the discussion of personal and social development for pupils and students with learning difficulties takes place within a debate about inclusion. Therefore the text includes a focus on personal and social development in many contexts – special schools, mainstream schools or special units. These assumptions arise from the idea that before we can plan personal and social education it is necessary to debate the two questions – What sort of persons are we educating for? and What sort of society? In this publication we will endeavour to give a theoretical justification and rationale for the work as well as demonstrating the practical application in current practice of these ideas and approaches.

So we have provided:

- a theoretical perspective;
- a selection of illustrative exemplars drawn directly from practice in a range of settings;
- reflections on the evolving role of education for personal and social development as part of the process of preparing learners for life in an increasingly inclusive society.

We hope that this text will encourage those in schools to look in an energetic way at their practice with a feeling that the examples and frameworks will support them in taking a critical and fresh look at matters.

Colleen McLaughlin
Richard Byers
Cambridge 2001

Terminology

In this book we have chosen to use the following terminology in the following ways and for the following reasons:

'Learning difficulties' is the phrase that we have used to describe the full range of severe, profound and multiple and moderate learning difficulties. Sometimes we have used a specific term because work has been developed for or written for a specific group.

We refer to 'pupils and students' because we wanted to cover the full 5 to 16 age range. Where we have specifically said 'pupils' or 'young people', it has been in order to emphasise relevance to a particular age group.

The word 'schools' is used to cover a range of provision, including mainstream and special schools in the maintained and independent sectors; units on and off mainstream sites; and some post-16 provision focused on the transition of young people with learning difficulties from school into further or adult continuing education.

Chapter 1

Personal and social development – the what and the why

There are many terms now in this territory of personal and social development. We shall use the phrases 'personal and social development' and 'personal and social education' and these are taken to include the emotional or affective as well as the health aspects of education. In this first chapter we will attempt to justify the focus on this aspect of education and put forward a framework for personal and social development.

> There is an abundance of evidence now to show that conscious understanding is not only unnecessary for many learning tasks, but may substantially interfere with learning.
> (Claxton 1999: 7)

This quotation shows the way in which the balance has shifted in debates about the cognitive, personal and social in learning and living. It is a sentence that will challenge many people's notions of learning. Weare (2000) argues that 19th- and early 20th-century reliance on the model of the rational human being is insufficient and shows that movements such as the feminist one have promoted a view of learning that acknowledges the part played by emotion. In psychology, philosophy and economics there is a shift in emphasis towards a greater acknowledgement of the role of the personal and social after an over-reliance on the cognitive. This is not an either/or debate but rather an acknowledgement that the part we have allocated to emotion and the personal/social has been too lowly. This shift is being argued for by people from many different spheres.

There has been an increasing interest in and emphasis on the socio-cultural aspects of learning. In the 1960s and 1970s Piagetian and cognitive accounts of learning were seen as the most significant.

> These theoretical traditions described cognitive development as a process of gradually emerging individual

Terminology

Shifting emphases

The personal and social aspects of learning

competencies. They also assume that intellectual development is stage-like and universal and that it occurs in pretty much the same way in all children in all cultural settings. They fail to acknowledge, however, the respects in which children's knowledge, skills, beliefs and understandings are socially constructed through talk and language and diverse processes of imitation, direct instruction, guided participation and collaborative construction.

(Faulkner *et al.* 1998:1)

So it has long been known that learning is personal and social but there is now an understanding that the personal and social elements play a bigger part than we have previously acknowledged.

Another example of a changing emphasis is in the extension of the notion of intelligence. Gardner (1993) has argued for multiple intelligences and Goleman (1996) for emotional intelligence in particular. Gardner (1993) argued that our conventional view of intelligence is limited. On the basis of a review of studies of individuals with exceptional capabilities in some areas and handicaps in others, he posited a framework of multiple intelligences: the linguistic, the logical-mathematical, the spatial, the musical, the bodily-kinaesthetic, the interpersonal and the intra-personal. Intra-personal intelligence is the ability to understand oneself, to reflect on self and to operate fully in life. Interpersonal intelligence is the ability to understand and communicate with others; as well as be able to collaborate with them and form effective relationships. He argued for the development of all these intelligences in schools and emphasised the need to create a climate for 'responsible learning'. However:

Bringing about such an environment is no easy matter. Individual students have a variety of needs, fears and aspirations and in such a world where many of the traditional supports have weakened, much of the burden for providing support falls on the school. Only if schools are concerned with civility, with fair treatment of all students from all groups, with feelings, interests, motivations and values as well as with cognitive goals, can such an environment be constructed and sustained.

(Gardner 1993)

Similarly, Goleman (1996) has demonstrated that those who achieve the greatest degree of success and satisfaction in their adult lives, both professionally and personally, are those who possess what he calls 'emotional intelligence'. By this he meant the ability to recognise emotions in others, handle relationships, manage emotions and know one's own emotions. These two writers are extending the notion of intelligence and of what we are educating for.

There is much research to show that the personal and social aspects of learning are inseparable from the cognitive. Rutter's (1992) research showed that the split between the academic and the personal/social dimensions of school was a false one. He demonstrated that schools needed to have both social and academic goals and that academic success, perseverance and self-esteem go hand in hand. Claxton (1999) has furthered this debate by arguing for the three Rs of learning power: resourcefulness, resilience and reflectiveness. Here, then, is an argument that the work of all teachers needs to include working with the emotional, social and personal in a more developmental way and with a more direct connection to learning of all kinds.

Students having a voice

These developments have been accompanied by an increasing awareness of the social and emotional world of schooling from the perspective of students. Indeed, some researchers have argued that listening to the student voice should be a central part of any strategy for school improvement (Rudduck *et al.* 1996). This has linked to recent debates about children's rights and the involvement of students in their school communities. The work of 'active citizenship' is a way in which many schools are likely to develop the work done in the territory of bullying and peer help (Cowie and Sharp 1996). This is also related to disability rights. The idea of students having a voice in their affairs both in and out of school is now well established.

Recent work undertaken by us has also shown that students want a dialogue with teachers and that the relationship and the communication around learning is central from the students' perspective (McLaughlin 2000). Students argued that the qualities and skills of good communication were the most important aspects of teaching for them. Skills and qualities mentioned were listening, respect, having a sense of humour and the all-encompassing 'communicates well'. This is a view of learning as relational and as such the personal and social aspects are inextricable from the cognitive.

Promoting mental and social health

The other set of concerns that drive the focus on the personal and social aspects of education are to do with social and mental health. For many decades the political debate centred on economics, particularly the economics of the market place, and the view that economics was unrelated to other disciplines. A healthy society was seen as one that was financially sound. There have been concerns about the inequalities and outcomes of an unregulated market (Hutton 1995). Lately the notion of 'social capital' has emerged. This is the idea that the economic health of a society is dependent on its social relations and communities. If trust breaks down between people and in communities then all relationships, including business ones, will suffer. So there has been a political shift towards emphasising social goals and processes in education.

3

In the field of mental health there have been concerns that the social changes that have taken place are causing problems. Weare (2000: 3) states that most societies are experiencing an increase in mental illness, crime, drug abuse and divorce. She argues that 'people have become more isolated from each other and that we are seeing a breakdown in communities and in traditional patterns of employment, along with an increase in urban alienation.' Although many might dispute aspects of the above arguments, there is clearly evidence that society is changing and that personal and social development is key to living in a changing and highly complex society where most established patterns are mutating. The debate about what sort of persons and what sort of society is desirable is one that is central to personal and social education. Pring (1984) has argued that we must make these values explicit and that this values debate is central to personal and social education. This is discussed further in Chapter Three. The values debate about the role of student and adults with learning and other disabilities is also picked up in the next chapter.

There is also a view that schools have a key role to play in responding to mental health concerns (WHO 1998). The concept of the health-promoting school has been developed over the last decade and the current Healthy Schools Initiative is the outcome of that in the UK. In other countries similar initiatives are being undertaken. In Australia there are initiatives such as 'MindMatters', which are focusing on the development of positive health among young people. Current concerns include a rise in depression and suicide among young people, high rates of teenage pregnancy and rising rates of sexually transmitted diseases. However, the approach being adopted by initiatives such as the Healthy Schools one is much more developmental and does not focus purely on responding to problems.

We have argued here that there has been a return to the prioritisation of personal and social development in education for a multitude of reasons: many to do with learning and mental and social health. It has been argued that this necessarily engages us in a values debate about what sort of persons we are aiming to educate and for what sort of society. It also engages us in thinking about and justifying a framework for that development.

A framework for personal and social development

A framework, which is rooted in adolescent development, is that of W. D. Wall (1977). He argued that adolescent development could be seen to include the development of the following aspects of self:

Bodily self

This area is about understanding and exploring physical development, as well as the use and care of the body and attitudes to the body. This would include areas such as gender and cultural issues related to the body and abuse of the body. The development of a positive body image and productive ways of caring for the body are part of this development. A healthy lifestyle is part of this.

Sexual self

This relates to sexual development, the role of sexuality and relationships. Students are entitled to have opportunities to gain information; to explore the more complex area of attitudes to sex and sexuality; to debate issues of power and control in sexual relations; and to explore pressures and prejudices.

Social self

Understanding others' perspectives and their role in relationships: making sense of others and their judgements; coping with conflicts; presenting oneself in a range of situations; and working with others are central themes here. The whole area of making friendships and other relationships is important here. On a wider level this is also about understanding the society in which we live and debating the values and workings of that society.

Vocational self

This area relates to a sense of purpose and meaningful occupation in life. It is also about developing an awareness of the roles we play in adult life. It is the all-important area of learning about transitions and the transitions we have to make

Philosophical self

This self is what Watkins (1995) has relabelled the moral or political self. It is related to the making of judgements and moral action. It is the area covered by citizenship as well as religious and moral education.

Hamblin (1978) and Watkins (1995) have added two further aspects:

Self as learner

This is the view of oneself as a learner and the process of reflecting on learning, achievement and progress. It includes learning about learning and the three Rs of Claxton (1999) – resourcefulness, resilience and refectiveness.

Self in the community of the school

This area is that of the person in the community of the school – students' learning in the community; their engagement with it; and making sense of and contributing to the school as a community.

This framework can help teachers to begin to generate a plan for the developmental needs of young people, to plan the curriculum, to begin to frame the purposes of their work and to think through where and how these areas are developed in the curriculum and school as a whole. We need also to allow for some flexibility in this curriculum – it is not just about the teachers' view, but it can be a useful starting point for discussion with students, parents and carers and other adults in the community of the school. The concepts of knowledge, skills and attitudes are applicable to this framework. It can be used to develop a curriculum for personal and social development. Within each area the knowledge, skills and attitudes need to be outlined as well as the values debated. Many of the current policy initiatives such as Healthy Schools Standard, PSHE and Citizenship can be mapped on to this framework. This approach gives all those engaged with personal and social development an opportunity to debate the aims of the work.

However, the planned learning offer of the curriculum is not the only place that personal and social development is taking place. All interactions in the school contribute to learning about self and others. I will learn a great deal from how adults and peers treat me, from their expectations of me, from the models they present and from the behaviours and attitudes I observe. One of the most important areas of personal and social development is peer relationships and peer learning. The ability to make satisfactory peer relationships or friendships is central to personal and social satisfaction and fulfilment as well as mental health. Work by Button (1974) has shown how important is the ability to form friendships in adolescence, and recent work by Dunn (1993) has shown that in newly constituted families friendships with peers is a key factor in developing resilience to stress and adversity. So this is a very important area.

The locations for this learning are many and can be reflected upon by adults that work in schools. It permeates all that is done and we have endeavoured to show that in this text. We will discuss personal and social development in the following arenas: the social context of the school; the curriculum; approaches to teaching and learning; and support for individual students through planning and monitoring.

Chapter 2

Inclusion and participation – the social context for personal and social development

This chapter addresses the key issue of the self in the community, referred to previously, and explores the proposition that the work of schools and colleges is underpinned by sets of values. We argue that these values should be made explicit for the benefit of all members of the school or college community. With Watkins (1995), we also suggest that where the ethos of the school or college is founded upon sound values, 'every occasion' in the teaching and learning day can make a positive contribution to pupils' and students' personal and social development.

Introduction

We will review the values which might underpin the curriculum in the light of the contribution this process might make to learners' personal and social development. We will consider the implications of this debate for those learners whom we describe here and throughout this book as having 'learning difficulties'. In using this and related terms, we emphasise our serious misgivings about their accuracy, objectivity or appropriateness but we acknowledge that, at this stage in the debate, we need to use readily understood terms in order to identify the learners about whom we are writing.

We will argue that the positive development of a sense of self in the community will depend upon:

- The extent to which pupils and students are encouraged and enabled to become active participants in teaching and learning;
- the inclusivity of schools and colleges, although we will use that term to cover more than locational mainstreaming and articulate a role for specialist provision in a more inclusive pattern of provision;
- the relationships that are fostered between staff and learners in and out of classroom settings and throughout the course of the teaching and learning day.

In these ways we will begin to focus on ways of promoting personal and social development for all learners, including those with learning difficulties currently working in specialist contexts.

Statements of values, aims and purposes

The revised National Curriculum (DfEE/QCA, 1999a) provides, for the first time, a statement of values and purposes underpinning the school curriculum. Interestingly, this set of values emphasises the whole curriculum and a broad set of aspects of selfhood that should be developed through education:

> Education is a route to the spiritual, moral, social, cultural, physical and mental development, and thus the well-being, of the individual.
>
> (page 10)

The values' and purposes' statement also emphasises fairness and equitability, along with notions about politics, economics and care for the environment:

> Education is also a route to equality of opportunity for all, a healthy and just democracy, a productive economy, and sustainable development.
>
> (page 10)

The National Curriculum makes it clear that the individual can make a contribution to these important movements but that the individual also operates in relation to other people both personally and socially. The National Curriculum statement of values and purposes argues that our responsibilities include:

> valuing ourselves, our families and other relationships, the wider groups to which we belong, the diversity in our society and the environment in which we live.
>
> (page 10)

According to the National Curriculum, education should 'reaffirm our commitment' to a set of core 'virtues', which are seen as 'enduring' through changing contexts, including 'truth, justice, honesty, trust and a sense of duty'. However, education must also enable us to be responsive to 'the opportunities and challenges of the rapidly changing world in which we live and work'. We are encouraged to consider the ways in which we need to prepare ourselves, 'as individuals, parents, workers and citizens' for the unknown future the world is moving towards in terms of, for example:

> economic, social and cultural change, including the continued globalisation of the economy and society, with new work and leisure patterns and with the rapid expansion of communication technologies.
>
> (page 10)

This could be seen as an interesting clarion call for those of us who work with young people with learning difficulties. It is certainly our intention, in writing this book, to emphasise some of the ways in which the curriculum for personal and social development can help young people with learning difficulties to prepare for the new opportunities we hope that their adult lives will hold for them 'as individuals, parents, workers and citizens'. We note with interest the statement of values and purposes in the National Curriculum and the ways in which it relates to previous work on the promotion of personal and social development as a core task for the curriculum (see, for example, Buck and Inman 1995). We also note that the National Curriculum statements about values and purposes are designed to include pupils and students with learning difficulties. According to the National Curriculum, the aims of the school curriculum are:

- to provide opportunities for all pupils to learn and to achieve;
- to promote pupils' spiritual, moral, social and cultural development and prepare all pupils for the opportunities, responsibilities and experiences of life.

(page 11)

As Byers (1998) suggests, such statements can be used as a basis for debate, in school and college communities, about ethos and about the foundations upon which the curriculum is constructed. We would argue that this process of bringing the notoriously intangible notion of ethos into the domain of the conscious and concrete by developing explicit statements about values and aims supports the key task of establishing a positive social context in which learning can take place. If this is important for all learners, it is arguably crucial for those who experience learning difficulties, since their futures, 'as individuals, parents, workers and citizens', are likely to be less certain, less predictable and more subject to change than those of many of their peers. Schools and colleges, we propose, must strive constantly to remain in touch with the developing options and realities, both optimistic and less encouraging, that the future holds for adults with learning difficulties.

In thinking through their values and their aims, school and college communities will need to ask themselves searching questions. These might include:

- Are the values and aims of our school or college explicit?
- Are members of the community, pupils, students, parents, staff and governors, and visitors made aware of these values and aims as they move around the school or college environment?
- Were these values and aims debated, negotiated and agreed with the involvement of all members of the school or college community, pupils, students, parents, staff and governors?
- What opportunities and challenges do we imagine society will present for pupils and students as they leave school or college and embark on their adult lives as individuals, parents, workers and citizens?

- Do we know how these opportunities and challenges are changing or how they may change in the longer term future?
- How are the values and aims of the school or college reviewed and revised in the light of these changing opportunities and challenges?
- How are all the members of the school or college community, students, parents, staff and governors, involved in this process of reviewing and revising values and aims?

Inclusive schools for inclusive societies

The proposed National Curriculum (DfEE/QCA 1999a) suggests that the values, aims and purposes we have discussed above can be put into practice most effectively if staff work in the context of three principles for inclusion. Before moving on to examine the statutory inclusion statement in the National Curriculum, we propose to explore the concept of inclusion, and its relationship with personal and social development for pupils and students with learning difficulties, in more depth.

As well as supporting practitioners in promoting the personal and social development of pupils and students with learning difficulties, we intend this book to make a contribution to the debate about inclusion. We suggest that working towards inclusion within a curriculum for all may be more appropriate, as an educative process, than emphasising access to, and presence in, one building rather than another. We will focus on promoting meaningful participation, progress and achievement for all within a range of learning experiences focused on inclusion in adult life beyond school and college. This is a goal which can be pursued in specialist contexts, and by specialist staff, as well as in the mainstream of education.

Identifying themes in the debate about inclusion

UNESCO produced its ground-breaking *Framework for Action on Special Educational Needs* in 1994 and the associated Salamanca statement (UNESCO 1994) is generally taken to be a key landmark in the debate about inclusion. Yet even in the relatively brief period of time since 1994, we have reached a situation where there are as many different definitions of inclusion as there are commentators – and there seem to be as many commentators as there are people with an interest, whether professional or personal, in the business of education.

We should first note that the idea of inclusion is clearly related to, yet not synonymous with, the concept of integration. In the UK in the 1970s and 1980s, integration entailed the assimilation of 'different' pupils as visitors or guests into 'host' mainstream schools and colleges, probably only for part of the time. Integration did not require either the mainstream settings or members of specialist communities to change their ways of thinking or their ways of doing things. Indeed, for some protagonists, integration was only viable if it had a minimal impact upon the status quo.

When considering the development of more inclusive practices in the post-16 sector, Tomlinson (FEFC 1996) argued that inclusion, compared with integration, is 'a larger and prior concept'. Integration, in crude summary, entails tinkering with aspects of the system in order to offer a less segregated experience for learners with special educational needs, providing that the system is not too upset by this process. Tomlinson's view of inclusion suggests something far more radical, challenging and potentially difficult to achieve.

Hall is, perhaps, among the more radical commentators on inclusion and, for Hall, inclusion can mean nothing less than full-time presence for all pupils in their local, neighbourhood, mainstream school. In 1996, for example, Hall argued that inclusion means:

> Being a full member of an age-appropriate class in your local school doing the same lessons as the other pupils and it mattering if you are not there. Plus you have friends who spend time with you outside school.
>
> (page 99)

Hall packs a number of elements into this brief statement. He uses the idea of 'full' membership of a class and, echoing Warnock's notion of 'functional integration', emphasises that this should entail 'doing the same lessons as the other pupils'. Hall suggests that all pupils, whatever their special educational needs, should be educated in their local schools with their age peers and geographical neighbours. He argues that the social dimension of inclusion, as well as the nature of the lessons themselves, is important.

Implementing Hall's 'mainstreaming for all' vision of inclusion would have a considerable impact on the status quo. But other interpretations of the notion of inclusion also entail change, often on a grand scale. Sebba and Ainscow (1996), for example, conceive of inclusion as a process whereby 'schools can be restructured in order to respond positively to all pupils as individuals'. Tomlinson's report (FEFC 1996) into inclusion in the post-16 sector advocates 'redesigning the very processes of learning, assessment and organisation so as to fit the objectives and learning styles of the students'. Clark *et al.* (1997) propose that this restructuring would entail 'a new and radical conceptualization of the relationship between the education of children "with special educational needs" and the nature of mainstream schools'. These authors' use of inverted commas suggests that they are as interested in a reconceptualisation of the conventional notion of 'special educational needs' as they are in restructuring the established nature of mainstream schooling. Jelly *et al.* (2000) pursue this theme. They define inclusion as:

> a process in which all members of the school community constantly challenge themselves to reconceptualise their policies, their practices, their roles and their perceptions

about the people around them in order to provide an ever more effective education for an ever more diverse range of learners.

(page 17)

This definition also emphasises the ongoing nature of the inclusion process. Inclusion is not an end state which it is possible to reach and to maintain. Inclusion is characterised, in Jelly *et al.*'s terms, by a commitment to a state of constant and continuing re-evaluation and revision of all the elements which, together, constitute schooling, wherever that schooling may take place.

Even if, as thinking about inclusion evolves, there is a retreat from the absolutist 'neighbourhood mainstream schooling for all' position advocated by commentators like Hall, there is still a sense in which developing a more inclusive educational system is liable to leave neither the mainstream of education nor the specialist sector unchanged. Some commentators argue that this process of change will, in itself, lead to improvement. Skrtic (1991), for example, proclaims that student diversity 'is an asset, an enduring source of uncertainty and thus the driving force behind innovation, growth of knowledge, and progress', suggesting that pupils and students with ever-more diverse needs should be welcomed into learning communities because, as agents of change, they provide the challenges which drive forward ongoing institutional improvement.

Focusing on participation

This certainly suggests that becoming more inclusive can have positive effects on the mainstream of education. Many commentators also emphasise the benefits of full participation for pupils and students with special educational needs. Florian (1998), in her definition of inclusion, emphasises the importance of participation in all areas of life, including education, when she argues that:

Inclusion refers to the opportunity for persons with a disability to participate fully in all of the educational, employment, consumer, recreational, community, and domestic activities that typify everyday society.

(page 16)

The authors of the influential *Index for Inclusion* (Booth *et al.* 2000) also emphasise participation as a key dimension in their multi-faceted definition of inclusion. Interestingly, these authors, with Sebba and Sachdev (1997), insist that inclusion must be actively concerned with reducing exclusion and that the school experience itself is cultural and social as well as purely educational. They suggest that:

Inclusion in education involves the processes of increasing the participation of students in, and reducing their exclusion from, the cultures, curricula and communities of local schools.

(page 12)

We would agree that participation is a key dimension in inclusive education and would suggest that it is also a key dimension in an education which is likely to promote effective personal and social development.

Exploring inclusive practices

The London Borough of Newham offers us some sense of what inclusive schooling in Hall's (1996) definition might look like. Colleagues in Newham have worked hard to ensure that as many pupils as possible attend schools in their immediate neighbourhoods. The Newham Inclusion Charter (Project Inclusion for Newham Council 1997) suggests that all pupils should have an opportunity to attend local schools. The Inclusion Charter proposes that all pupils, and their families, will be welcomed and valued for the diversity they bring to these local schools. According to the Charter, all pupils, whatever their individual needs, will be included in all the activities of the school communities in their locality. This approach can be exciting and powerful. Staff at Cleves School have documented some of their experiences in a book edited by Alderson (1999).

However, the Newham Inclusion Charter does also acknowledge that specialist expertise exists and that the inclusion of a greater diversity of pupils in the full life of a school community requires special effort. The Charter itself promotes the importance of special educational policy and practice and, in Newham, some of this expertise can be found in schools where additional or specialist resources and expertise, focused on supporting pupils with particular kinds of shared needs, are concentrated. This strategy acknowledges the possibility that not all pupils, all of the time, can be effectively educated strictly in their neighbourhood school.

The government's recent *Programme of Action* in relation to special educational needs (DfEE 1998) picks up many of these points. In a chapter devoted to developing a more inclusive education system, the DfEE presents a challenge to all mainstream schools to 'become as inclusive as possible'; to ensure 'equal treatment of children with SEN'; and to reduce rates of exclusion. However, the government's approach is to 'be practical, not dogmatic' and the chapter notes that there will continue to be a need for specialist provision, both in order to 'maximise choice for parents and pupils' and to ensure that the 'needs of individual children' are put first.

The DfEE has a vision of a more inclusive future in which 'the normal presumption is that children spend as much time as possible in a mainstream setting' but where specialist input continues to be available when such provision is deemed to be 'right for a child'. Specialist provision, in the form of special schools, units and specialist staff, will, argues the DfEE, 'continue to play a vital role' in a more inclusive future but the DfEE insists that specialist provision, just as much as the mainstream of education, has to change. Furthermore, the DfEE wants the specialist sector to be proactive about this change rather than waiting for the mainstream to lead progress towards a more inclusive future. The specialist sector must make and maintain close links with the mainstream so that it becomes 'much more closely integrated into local patterns of provision'. This will enable staff in both special and mainstream contexts to work much more closely together for the benefit of all pupils.

This proactive role will require special schools and units to: become 'confident, outward-looking centres of excellence' which provide short-term placements for pupils; work more closely with mainstream colleagues in order to plan support; share responsibility for pupils with mainstream schools; and develop roles as sources of 'expertise, advice and professional development for mainstream colleagues'. This, taken together with the TTA's recent standards for specialist teachers (1999), suggests new roles for specialist staff as well.

In order to move towards 'an increasingly inclusive education system', building on the strengths already established within the specialist sector, the DfEE does not have one simple template for development. Indeed, the *Programme of Action* suggests that inclusion is not a definable 'fixed state' but an ongoing process in which participants strive towards two key goals: 'higher standards of achievement for all' in education and, ultimately, the development of an 'inclusive society'. The DfEE chooses to illustrate aspects of this ongoing process in a variety of ways. Thus, for the DfEE (1988), working towards a more inclusive future might mean:

- 'placement of pupils with SEN in mainstream schools';
- 'the participation of young people in the full range of social experiences and opportunities once they have left school';
- 'the participation of all pupils in the curriculum and social life of mainstream schools';
- 'the participation of all pupils in learning which leads to the highest possible level of achievement'.

It is worth noting, in the terms of the *Programme of Action* at least, that the specialist sector can make highly significant contributions towards all of these ideals.

Three principles for inclusion in the National Curriculum

The new National Curriculum inclusion statement backs up these last two possibilities. The revised National Curriculum (DfEE/QCA 1999a) places a strong emphasis on providing effective learning opportunities for all learners. Three principles for more inclusive practice are established whereby practitioners set suitable learning challenges for all pupils; respond to pupils' diverse learning needs; and overcome potential barriers to learning and assessment for individuals and groups of pupils. In a little more detail, setting suitable learning challenges may mean:

- using the age-related programmes of study for the National Curriculum where possible in planning work for learners, but choosing work from earlier or later key stages when required to enable individual pupils to make progress or show what they can achieve;
- realising that this may mean that it will not be possible to cover all aspects of the age-related programmes of study;
- using the content of the programmes of study as a resource or to provide a context for learning which is appropriate to the age and requirements of pupils.

Responding to pupils' diverse learning needs may entail:

- setting high expectations for all;
- planning so that all pupils can take part;
- taking specific action to:
  - create effective learning environments;
  - secure motivation and concentration;
  - provide equality of opportunity through teaching approaches;
  - use appropriate assessment approaches;
  - set targets for learning.

Overcoming potential barriers to learning and assessment for individuals and groups of pupils will involve supporting participation, perhaps by using special arrangements which, for pupils with special educational needs, will include:

- differentiating tasks and materials;
- working with other agencies;
- providing access by:
  - providing help with communication, language and literacy, for example, by using information and communication technology or other alternative or augmentative modes of communication;
  - encouraging the use of all the senses and experiences available to a pupil, for example, sight, touch, sound, taste or smell and play, drama, visits and exploration of environment;
  - planning for full participation in learning and in physical and practical activities, for example, making use of aids, staff support, adaptations and alternative resources;

  – helping pupils to manage their behaviour, to take part in learning and to prepare for work, for example, by providing a clear structure and teaching pupils to work with others and independently;
  – helping pupils to manage their emotions, for example, by building self-esteem through positive feedback; allowing time for pupils to engage with learning; and increasing demands gradually.

The general requirements section of the National Curriculum (DfEE/QCA 1999a) also provides specific notes on overcoming potential barriers to learning and assessment for pupils with disabilities and for pupils who are learning English as an additional language.

Preparing for an inclusive society

It is worth noting here, as an issue which will be explored in more depth later in this book, that the non-statutory guidelines on teaching personal, social and health education provided in the National Curriculum handbooks (DfEE/QCA 1999a) are themselves designed to be inclusive and to apply to all pupils. In our view, there are many ways in which an inclusive school is likely also to be a school which promotes development for its pupils and students personally and socially. We summarise these relationships below:

- Pursuing the process of becoming more responsive to a greater diversity of pupils and students will:
  – improve schools and colleges for all;
  – enhance educational and societal inclusion;
  – contribute to pupils' and students' personal and social development as they learn to become members of increasingly diverse groups.

- Participation for all in more inclusive learning experiences and environments will promote inclusion in society beyond schools and colleges and therefore facilitate pupils' and students' personal and social development.

- The willingness of schools and colleges to change in order to promote participation and respond effectively to an ever-greater diversity of learners will also help those schools and colleges to continue to support pupils and students in preparing to engage with a constantly changing set of challenges in adult life.

- The willingness of all those engaged in the processes of becoming more inclusive to alter their perceptions about their work and about learners will help them constantly to challenge their preconceptions about the opportunities and possibilities that adult life might hold in store for pupils and students with learning difficulties.

Soon after the introduction of the original National Curriculum, Sebba *et al.* (1993) argued for 'some profound changes in the ways that many schools make provision for pupils with learning difficulties'. They proposed a reconsideration of accepted, historical power relationships between staff and pupils and students with learning difficulties in order to develop contexts for learning which promote 'empowerment and liberation rather than remediation and normalization'. Mittler (1996) regarded this stance as representing a 'radical departure' from established ways of thinking about schooling for pupils with learning difficulties. This departure required, from staff, 'innovative thinking' as advocated by Hart (1996) and a significant change in attitudes towards people with disabilities. Mittler (1996) made explicit links between this shift in thinking and the emerging perspectives of adults with disabilities as expressed through the advocacy and disability rights movements. We would wish to pursue this agenda in the pages of this book, encouraging staff in schools and colleges to move away from models of learning difficulties which focus on deficits; narrow concepts about achievements that people with learning difficulties 'can't do'; goals that are seen as 'unattainable'; and experiences that are regarded as 'inappropriate' for some learners. We do not propose that this shift in attitudes will be achieved in one clean conversion to new ways of thinking. Like the process of becoming more inclusive, it will be ongoing, messy, complex and continually challenging.

However if, as educationalists who work with young people with learning difficulties, we have learned anything from the introduction and assimilation of the National Curriculum, it must surely be that anything is possible. We propose here that we need to continue to move away from ideas about pupils with learning difficulties that place arbitrary limits on their learning and that impose barriers or boundaries, however rational these may seem at the time. We agree with some of the commentators on inclusion, noted above, who suggest that the language of special educational needs may prevent us from moving away from unhelpful concepts and models of learning difficulty. We would want to challenge, for example, notions about 'low IQ', 'mental age' or 'developmental age'. To regard a learner as being diminished in these ways is likely to lead to the provision of narrow, impoverished experiences. Why would staff working with students whom they regard as being 'developmentally young', for example, seek to provide a preparation for the opportunities and challenges of adulthood? With Griffiths (1994), we argue for learners, and their parents and professional enablers, to be emancipated from the restricting influences of these forms of thinking. However, we do not want to encourage staff simply to pretend that learning difficulties of one kind or another do not exist. To deny the objectively verifiable impairments experienced by some learners is surely as unhelpful as being constrained by

Developing positive attitudes

stereotypical assessments of those things that learners in certain categories 'cannot', or should not, do. We would therefore encourage staff:

- constantly to challenge and question the categorical terms that are used to describe learners and the educational implications that appear logically to flow from them;
- to assess learners' difficulties honestly and accurately and to consider their implications for full participation in education;
- to work with learners, their families, enablers and advocates in order to look for positive ways forward in overcoming, minimising, circumventing or compensating for those difficulties in order to promote inclusion and personal and social development.

Sebba *et al.* (1993) and Byers (1998) agree that the process of emancipation to which Griffiths (1994) refers will involve a searching re-evaluation of systems, procedures, personal constructs and attitudes on the part of staff. These authors discuss the importance of monitoring the impact of a range of factors on pupils' and students' personal and social development. These factors include:

- rules, routines and rituals running through the school and college day;
- moment-by-moment relationships between staff and learners, including approaches to the provision of help, support and guidance; and ways of offering praise and rewards.

Reconsidering rules, routines and rituals

All learners find themselves subject to rules. Pupils and students with learning difficulties, however, often work in contexts where there are relatively few explicit rules. Staff may suggest that having too many rules can lead to confusion or that rules are difficult to communicate to pupils and students with learning difficulties. We suggest that more recent developments are exploring the challenge of involving pupils and students with learning difficulties more effectively in negotiating, agreeing, implementing and reviewing rules and codes of conduct for the learning situation. These initiatives build on practices that are relatively familiar in the mainstream of education (see, for example, Rogers, 1991; and Mosley, 1996). Authors like Jelly *et al.* (2000) report on pupil involvement in individual and class contexts and, with Winup (1994), also describe active pupil participation in school councils and committees. In gathering views in preparation for writing this book, we heard about examples of practice in which members of the school council had the right, each year, collectively to discuss and agree targets which were then written into and enacted via the school development plan. Mittler (1996) suggests that being a member of such committees, and realising that their work has a real impact, can help pupils and students with learning difficulties to learn important lessons about agency and advocacy. We contend that these processes will also have an important impact upon pupils' and students' personal and social development.

Pupils and students with learning difficulties may have relatively few explicit rules to live by but may find themselves operating according to a large number of implicit or hidden codes of conduct. These codes are often embedded in routines and rituals which are revisited at certain parts of the day or week. Staff will suggest that these routines and rituals are particularly important for pupils and students with learning difficulties for a number of reasons, for example:

- they help to provide and to emphasise a clear structure for the day for those learners who prefer to operate within established patterns of behaviour;
- they externalise structure for those who find it difficult to internalise sequences of activity;
- they offer opportunities for pupils and students to become attuned to predictable outcomes and consequences in familiar circumstances;
- they provide a sense of safety and security for those learners who experience the world as being full of unpredictable changes;
- they reinforce messages about consistency of response in contexts in which events and staff behaviours are themselves consistent;
- they offer regular opportunities to maintain and refine developing skills.

While we would not deny these positive aspects of repeated activities, we would suggest that routines and rituals can lose their meaning and become rigid. Pupils and students who have begun to learn about structure, predictability and consistency may need to have their emerging confidence tested against changes in routine. Learners whose skills are beginning to be established may require opportunities to transfer and generalise those skills into new situations. Pupils and students who have learned to trust the security of a sheltered environment have the right to explore their responses to a real world which is comparatively challenging and unpredictable. For these reasons, we propose, routines and rituals should be subjected to constant reappraisal as part of the process of driving forward pupils' and students' personal and social development.

Promoting positive relationships between staff and learners

In our discussion of attitudes towards learning difficulties and disabilities, we have already touched upon the importance of the relationship between teacher and learner. Sebba *et al.* (1993) and Byers (1998) take this debate further by suggesting that familiar staff approaches that involve the routine provision of help, support and guidance can 'lead to dependence and the denial of autonomy'. In order to help staff promote independence and interdependence rather than dependence, we provide, in Figure 2.1, a series of questions which can be used in order to re-evaluate supporting relationships.

Is the support always provided by the same member of staff?

Do members of staff have their 'special' pupils with whom they work most of the time?

Is support provided by peers: never? sometimes? often? all the time?

Does the support pupils receive promote access to and participation in the learning activities experienced by the majority of peers?

Does the nature of the support provided take pupils away from the mainstream flow of activities and experiences: never? sometimes? often? all the time?

Is the support focused on helping a pupil? Or on overcoming a particular difficulty, perhaps in a particular session?

Is the support focused on helping one pupil? Or on supporting learning across all the members of a group?

Do pupils have opportunities to work independently: never? sometimes? often? all the time?

Do pupils have opportunities to make mistakes and solve problems: never? sometimes? often? all the time?

Do pupils have opportunities to take risks, within the parameters of a carefully constructed risk-taking policy: never? sometimes? often? all the time?

Figure 2.1 Evaluating support

The use of help, support and guidance, while it can be positive, has to be subject to scrutiny if the most effective approaches to fostering learners' personal and social development are to be assured. In the same way, we suggest, the use of praise and rewards has to be maintained under review. In the past, staff working with pupils with learning difficulties learned the value of positive praise and systems involving the liberal use of tangible rewards from their training in the behavioural tradition (see, for example, McBrien and Foxen 1981). Some authors (for example, Zarkowska and Clements 1994) suggest that a reward can be used 'without any problems', providing it meets certain criteria for effectiveness, and that, if a person becomes satiated with a reward, a selection of alternative rewards can be 'delivered on a random basis' in order to overcome this difficulty. We would not wish to challenge these assertions in the context of carefully ordered behaviour management protocols, but we do suggest that the wholesale adoption of attitudes like this towards praise and reward in the classroom can have an undesirable impact upon pupils' and students' personal and social development. Learners do need to understand, and to feel, that their achievements are recognised, honestly appraised and celebrated in appropriate ways, but they should not be encouraged to perform solely for reward; to conform to adult expectations simply in order to attain positive reinforcement; or to expect a constant supply of adult attention and praise in response to their every action. It is possible for pupils and students to learn to function only in the context of tangible rewards and adult attention and this is clearly unhelpful when it is hoped that learners will ultimately become as independent as possible. We suggest that praise from staff and extrinsic rewards should be used in careful balance with a range of other forms of motivation including:

- the recognition of achievements by members of the peer group;
- self-assessment, self-review and self-validation;
- the celebration and accreditation of achievement by those outside the teaching and learning situation, including families and external validators;
- a sense of the intrinsic value of purposeful and engaging activity.

Closing comments

We suggest that the social context in which teaching and learning take place should, like other aspects of the work of schools and colleges, be maintained under regular and rigorous review in order to ensure that opportunities to promote personal and social development among pupils and students are maximised. We propose that this is particularly important where pupils and students experience learning difficulties. Societal attitudes or lack of access may restrict the opportunities available to these learners. We have noted the availability of a number of evaluative tools (Booth *et al.* 2000; Project Inclusion for Newham Council 1997) which we commend to practitioners committed to the notion of promoting personal and social development for all.

In the next chapter of this book, we turn to the notion of the planned curriculum for personal and social education and offer guidance on making policy, planning and review. The examples we use to illustrate the issues in these chapters will help to focus our earlier discussions of the development of a range of aspects of selfhood in learners and will support staff in taking account of the learning potential of the full range of experiences in the school or college day as well as planning lessons focused on personal and social education.

Chapter 3

Personal and social development in schools

The personal and social development of children is one way of describing the central purpose of education.

(HMI 1979: 206)

This statement from HMI is interesting for two reasons. First, it says something about scale – the area of personal and social development can be so huge that it slips from the grasp since it can be so all encompassing. Second, that since 1979 there has been a shift in views of 'the central purpose of education'. The priority became the National Curriculum and the core curriculum – that is changed and now there is a need to reconsider the territory and to justify it. In this chapter we will begin by looking at the history of personal and social education in the school context and then develop the justification.

The development of personal and social education in schools

Although schools have always been involved with the personal and social development of students, the term personal and social education is a recent one in the history of educational terminology. It was in the 1970s that personal and social education courses began to appear on school timetables. This was part of a change in thinking about the relationship of schools and teachers to the personal and social issues of students. Up until the 1970s teachers had taken rather a reactive role in this area. They had reacted to the problems that students brought to school often in a largely individual way. Counselling and guidance courses for teachers had begun to appear in higher education and they reflected the idea that teachers and schools should respond to students' individual welfare and personal/social concerns. It was a problem-based approach and this is still an issue in personal and social education provision.

In the 1970s there was a shift to a more educative and preventative approach. There were some major curriculum developments and many courses were produced for schools. Examples of these were Active Tutorial Work (Baldwin and Wells 1979–83) or the work of Hamblin (1978) and Hopson and Scally (1981). Personal and social education courses often included sex education, life-skills education, careers education, drugs and alcohol education and social education. The development of these courses was lead by teachers in schools, rather than external bodies. There was a gradual realisation that this approach also had problems. The courses were seen as too problem-focused, i.e. they were often a response to a list of the major hurdles and problems that adolescents might encounter. For example there would be lessons on getting pregnant, drug misuse and so on. Courses could become a 'pot pourri of topics' (Pring 1984) and have little coherence or rationale.

There was also a concern that personal and social education was becoming reduced to providing a course and that this was leading to a fragmented approach where the development of the personal and social aspects of education was being reduced and separated from the rest of the curriculum. In special schools similar concerns were being expressed and the equation of personal and social education with self-help skills was an additional concern (Sebba *et al.* 1993). However, this was part of the development of curricula and these criticisms could be seen as bringing a more critical approach to the field.

So there was a concern to make personal and social education more developmental and educative in its responses. The need for a clear rationale was also shown, as well as the need to improve the status of this area of the curriculum. Initiatives such as the Technical and Vocational Education Initiative (TVEI) had enhanced the status of personal and social education, moving it more to the centre of the stage. Then in 1988 the National Curriculum was introduced. The previous developments in personal and social education were not mirrored in the proposed new curriculum. In fact in the initial consultative document it was not mentioned at all. There was also a fierce political debate about the values in education. Personal and social education was seen as central to the values' debate and became a real focus of change. The developments in the 1980s and 1990s will be explored next.

The National Curriculum and personal and social education

Section 1 of the Education Reform Act 1988 stated that schools had a statutory responsibility to provide 'a broad and balanced curriculum' which 'promotes the pupil's spiritual, moral, cultural, mental and physical development and prepares pupils for the opportunities, responsibilities and experiences of adult life'. This was restated in the 1996 Education Act and still holds today. However the initial proposals for the National Curriculum did not place much emphasis on personal and social education. The eventual conception was of personal and social education as cross-curricular dimensions, themes and skills (NCC 1989). However this was in a context of great emphasis on subjects and the imposition of cross-curricular dimensions, themes and skills on top of, or in opposition to, a subject-based curriculum already defined in great detail was problematic, despite the document describing these changes being entitled *The Whole Curriculum*. It was post hoc planning and was a case of shutting the stable door after the curriculum horse had bolted.

The definition of the cross-curricular dimensions and themes was as follows. The cross-curricular dimensions were 'personal and social education, equal opportunities and multicultural education' (NCC 1989: 1.3). These were described as 'interwoven in to the curriculum, both formal and informal' whereas the cross-curricular themes were listed as 'health education, environmental education and economic and industrial understanding' (NCC 1989: 1.3). They were said to be 'less pervasive than the cross-curricular dimensions' and were said to have 'a strong component of knowledge and understanding in addition to skills' (NCC 1989). By 1990 the five themes were:

- economic and industrial understanding;
- careers education and guidance;
- health education;
- education for citizenship; and
- environmental education.

(NCC 1990a)

It was claimed that these themes were seen as 'pre-eminent' by 'most people' and inevitably because of the detailed specification of the content of these themes they came mistakenly, but understandably, to be seen as *the* definition of the curriculum for personal and social education. There were also cross-curricular skills, such as problem-solving, personal and communication skills. These are linked to current conceptions of 'key skills' but since guidance was promised and never materialised, this area of provision soon lost focus. The reader can be forgiven for feeling confused regarding all these themes, dimensions and skills. As has already been said, the themes were the most clearly specified and therefore they were more readily understood and accepted.

However, there is evidence that the cross-curricular approach did not succeed and added to the already diminished status of personal and social education, despite the fact that they were well received in the specialist sector (Ashdown *et al.* 1991). The issue of coherence and rationale was also still there.

> Cross-curricular issues and personal and social development do not have coherence of purpose or a high profile in the curriculum at the present time, despite schools' abiding interest in these matters. The requirements of the National Curriculum, assessment pressures and accountability weaken the place of cross-curricular issues.
>
> (Ford *et al.* 1998)

Watkins (1999) identifies other effects of the National Curriculum on personal and social education. He argues that it is teacher dominated, i.e. it 'all too often reflects the adults' anxieties, current moral panics or the latest set of resources from an interest group' (p. 77). He argues that there is a lack of connectedness in the school curriculum and in personal and social education.

So at the beginning of the 21st century the concerns about the development of personal and social education can be summed up thus. First, that the whole field of personal and social education had become reduced to the provision of a course. 'We still see it as schemes of work', said a head teacher in the focus group we held. Second, that these courses were often based on a random series of topics or were problem-based. So the lack of a rationale for the curriculum in this area had been established. Third, that there was fragmentation in the approach and there was a lack of 'connectedness' in the curriculum. Fourth, that for these and other reasons, such as the subject approach embodied in the National Curriculum, personal and social education did not have high status in schools. Before going on to examine the latest proposal for this area in Curriculum 2000 and other initiatives let us look at the issues in justifying and defining personal and social education.

Defining personal and social education

A broad and useful definition of personal and social education is that used by Watkins (1999), 'the intentional promotion of the personal and social development of pupils through the whole curriculum and the whole school experience'. However, the minute we step in to the territory we are engaged, either implicitly or explicitly, in views of what sort of persons and what sort of society we are educating for and what we mean by personal and social development (Pring 1984). This values debate is important and often invisible. A recent tendency has been to avoid this debate and to suggest that values are 'self evident' (NCC 1990a). In our view, to do this diminishes the importance of personal and social education.

As part of the process of compiling this book, we held a small group discussion on 'What is personal and social education?' with six head teachers of special schools. This discussion will be used to illustrate some of the questions and dilemmas.

Values and personal and social education

When asked to define or give a conception of what PSE meant to them, the head teachers immediately came up with words like 'behaviour', 'social relationships', 'skills for living', 'independent skills' and 'citizenship'. What was immediately prompted was discussion around the values of society and the aims of those working with students with learning difficulties. In other words the first questions are: What sort of society? and What sort of persons? The debate in the group immediately got in to this territory. Do we educate for conformity or for change? There was a recognition that we need to accept the socialising function that we as educators have but also at the same time to go beyond that.

Models of personal and social education

In the views in the discussion there were elements of different models of personal and social education. Some of the views mirrored those identified by Sebba *et al.* in 1993, who linked Ryder and Campbell's (1988) work on PSE in mainstream schools with models of the curriculum in special education. Sebba *et al.* identified four main models. The first model they identified as the deficit model, which identifies the deficits in students and then attempts to remedy them. This has been described as the *medical or transitional model*. In terms of PSE this model can be recognised as the problem-based curriculum which identifies all the possible pitfalls or problems in life and devises a topic-based curriculum to remedy this. So the topics of sex and drugs can dominate such a curriculum. This model was not one that was identified by the head teachers but it is a common one underpinning many curricula.

A model that was alluded to was the *individual model* of care and PSE. This model emphasises the individual and his or her needs. It can emphasise the fulfilling of the potential of students and an emphasis on education that recognises:

> that our pupils are individual human beings in their own right and they have needs, desires, drive. They have emotions like any other pupil who has not got disabilities and those kids will actually throughout the course of the day, experience order and excitement, anger, fright and so and so forth.
>
> (Head teacher in discussion)

It can be a demanding sense of the individual as both the 'authentic author of their own experience' (head teacher in discussion) but also as responsible for their actions. 'PSE is allowing the pupils or students to fully realise, as much as they can, that they are totally responsible for their own experience' (head teacher in discussion). In this model the curriculum can be devised by addressing the individual needs of the students. Issues raised here include: the balance between individual needs and responsibility to others; who decides what the individual needs are; and whether students with disabilities are always perceived as in need of 'care'.

A third model was described by Sebba *et al.* (1993) as the *educational or rational model*. This model at its weakest is the 'filling of empty vessels' model where students are seen as empty and with no personal and social learning to bring to their education. At its strongest this model emphasises learning and the role of the school as a site for personal and social development. Here the educational role of the school is emphasised by a head teacher: 'It is the skills that children need to have in order to learn'. The skills identified in the discussion group were social skills and communication skills.

Finally, the social aspects were emphasised in the discussion group and this could be identified as a more *radical or partnership* approach. Here the talk was of advocacy and changing society, the use of social power and assertiveness. The debate also raised issues of roles and responsibilities.

So the starting point for personal and social education is how do we answer this question: What sort of society and what sort of persons are we aiming to develop? This question does not imply omnipotence or the false suggestion that schools are totally responsible for students' development. Personal and social development is complex and something that occurs in all the settings in our lives, not just school. However, schools are powerful contributors. Rutter (1991) has shown how powerful the school's contribution to later adult life can be. If the school takes social and personal goals seriously then this can affect young people's lives in many spheres later – as parents, as partners and as workers.

In clarifying the values and goals for personal and social education it is likely that we will take elements from all the models previously referred to. We have to manage the tensions and dilemmas inherent in that debate and we also have to question the entitlements and limits of our curriculum.

We need to bring coherence and continuity to the curriculum. It also needs an educational justification. In Chapter One we argued for a framework based on the work of W. D. Wall (1977) who argued that adolescent development was about the formation of a sense of identity and that this included the development of the following aspects of self:

A framework for personal and social development

- bodily self;
- sexual self;
- social self;
- vocational self;
- philosophical self;
- self as learner;
- self in the community of the school.

This area is that of the person in the community of the school – their learning from that; their engagement with it; and their making sense of and contributing to the school as a community.

This framework can help teachers to begin to generate a plan for the developmental needs of young people, to plan the curriculum, to begin to frame the purposes of our work and to think through where and how these areas are developed in the curriculum and school as a whole. We need also to allow for some flexibility in this curriculum – it is not just about the teachers' view, but this can be a useful starting point for discussion with students, parents and carers and other adults in the community of the school. Guidelines on planning, teaching and assessing the curriculum stress 'that there are no nationally specified times for particular subjects. It is for schools to determine and justify the amount of time allocated to different parts of their curriculum over the course of a week, a term, a year or a key stage' (QCA 2001a). Teachers are encouraged to meet the needs of pupils in their settings and to emphasise particular parts of the curriculum. It is hoped that the framework outlined here will encourage in-depth and creative planning of personal and social development through the curriculum, rather than a narrower more reactive approach which consists solely of following government guidelines.

Learning and teaching

It has already been pointed out that we do not just learn from one location. The evidence is that the 'what' and the 'how' of learning in this area of personal and social development are inseparable. All the evidence on personal and social learning emphasises the experiential nature of it and this is even more likely to be the case where students employ more non-verbal forms of learning. We make meaning from the events occurring in our lives – planned and unplanned. This learning is then reflected on and transferred or not to the next situation. So as a young person how I am treated physically when I am being taken to the toilet or given physical care will have a huge impact on my bodily self. Equally, the expectations that people operate on will shape my learning too. So all that occurs in the school day will impact on my personal and social development and learning about myself and the world I inhabit. We are constantly making meaning.

Vygotsky (Haste 1999) saw 'the individual as an active agent, making sense and constructing meaning within a social and cultural environment' (p. 182). He posited that there was a 'zone of proximal development', arguing that 'concepts first come to the attention of the individual through interpersonal action and discussion: only later are they internalised by the individual' (Haste 1999: 183). So the learning is located in the interaction between teacher and student. Or as one head teacher put it 'I think that the place where the knowledge about who that person is really generated is in the classroom and it is in the relationship and that is why the stuff on intensive interaction and empathy for the learner is important'. So personal and social development is located in all the interactions in the school, in the relationship, in the formal curriculum and in the out-of-class experiences in school. In Chapter Five, approaches to teaching and learning are discussed in full. But first let us go on to look at current policy on personal and social education.

Chapter 4

The curriculum for personal and social education

Part one: current policy on personal and social education

There has been much activity recently in the field of personal and social education. The National Curriculum was reviewed and Curriculum 2000 was the result, with PSHE and Citizenship firmly on the agenda again. The other major initiative is the Healthy Schools initiative or the National Healthy School Standard (DfEE 1999a). We will look in detail at these initiatives as well as the other related areas such as sex education and work-related learning. It is clearly to be welcomed that there is this restating of personal and social education as important, even if it is possible to be cynical about the instrumental purposes of the political shift. In terms of accountability it has a high priority. The OFSTED *Handbook for Inspecting Special Schools and Pupil Referral Units* (OFSTED 1999) places PSHE alongside English and mathematics as priority areas of the curriculum.

The proposals in the National Curriculum are as follows:

Personal, social and health education (PSHE)/citizenship

- PSE is non-statutory but there are guidelines for it and it is seen as an entitlement under the legal requirement of preparation for adult life and for a broad and balanced curriculum that includes social, moral spiritual and cultural education (DfEE/QCA 1999a and DfEE 1999a). There are also separate guidelines for those working with students with learning difficulties (QCA/DfEE 2001a).
- There are frameworks for PSHE and Citizenship at Key Stages 1 and 2 and for PSHE at Key Stages 3 and 4. They are included as non-statutory guidelines in the National Curriculum handbooks.

A summary of proposals in Curriculum 2000

- A new foundation subject in Citizenship at Key Stages 3 and 4 will become statutory from August 2002. Citizenship is non-statutory at Key Stages 1 and 2.
- **Sex education** is statutory and new guidance was issued in 2000 (DfEE 2000a)
- **Careers education** is statutory in Years 9, 10 and 11
- **Religious education** is statutory
- **Key skills** are statutory. They are the skills of communication, the application of number, information technology, working with others, improving learning and performance and problem solving.
- **Inclusion**

A new statutory statement on providing effective learning opportunities for all pupils replaces the current statutory statements on access. The new statement sets out three key principles for inclusion:

- setting suitable learning challenges;
- responding to pupils' diverse learning needs;
- overcoming potential barriers to learning and assessment for individuals and groups of pupils.

A detailed process of evaluating educational inclusion has also been produced and the issue of inclusion and exclusion has definitely risen on the accountability ladder (OFSTED 2001). Schools need to take action at all levels of curriculum planning to ensure that provision is made to meet the individual requirements. Let us now examine these proposals in more detail.

Personal, social and health education (PSHE) and citizenship

The framework for PSHE (DfEE/QCA 1999b) stresses the importance of PSHE, as do the guidelines for pupils with learning difficulties. Past experience in this field would suggest that the areas of PSHE and citizenship should be as fully integrated as possible to avoid the fragmentation that has occurred in this territory in the past. There are five main areas of development in the framework and guidelines: they are:

Developing confidence and responsibility and making the most of one's abilities

This area highlights working with self – the self-concept, self-awareness, self-esteem and self-knowledge. The aim of work here according to the guidelines is the development of a positive self-image, the development of the ability to communicate needs, feelings and opinions and the development of the ability to take responsibility for oneself.

Preparing to play an active role as citizens (Key Stages 1 and 2) and developing knowledge and understanding about becoming informed citizens (Key Stages 3 and 4)

In the Crick Report (QCA 1998), on which the citizenship proposals are based, there are three main elements that run through this conceptualisation of citizenship (QCA 2000). These are:

Social and moral responsibility:

'Children learning from the very beginning self-confidence and socially and morally responsible behaviour both in and beyond the classroom, both towards those in authority and towards each other' (QCA 1998).

Community involvement:

'Learning about and becoming helpfully involved in the life and concerns of their communities, including learning through community involvement and service to the community' (QCA 1998);

Political literacy:

'Pupils learning about how to make themselves effective in public life through knowledge, skills and values – what can be called "political literacy"' (QCA 1998).

Key concepts in education for citizenship are according to QCA (2000):

- democracy and autocracy;
- cooperation and conflict;
- equality and diversity;
- fairness, justice, the rule of law and human rights;
- freedom and order;
- the individual and the community;
- power and authority;
- rights and responsibilities.

These are all very real issues for pupils with learning difficulties and raise issues about inclusion. They also have portent outside of the curriculum and many schools have done excellent work around the involvement of students and listening to the student voice in school.

The associated guidelines (QCA/DfEE 2001a) state that, in the context of students with learning difficulties, the aim regarding the development of active citizens is to help pupils 'move from a personal view of themselves and their immediate world, towards a much wider perspective'. This is about decision making and involvement in the community of the school and the wider community. Moral education and issues of boundaries are part of this work. The guidelines state that teaching this aspect across the Key Stages can help pupils to:

- make choices;
- take part in group activities;
- recognise differences and similarities in people.

These are not new areas of the curriculum for pupils with learning difficulties but the balance of the curriculum has often tended towards the first two themes of citizenship and the challenge will be to see how the third theme can be developed.

Developing a healthy lifestyle

This area is about a safe and healthy lifestyle. The guidelines (QCA/DfEE 2001a) state that this aspect of the curriculum aims to help pupils to:

- learn about the need for personal hygiene, take part in and maintain personal hygiene routines;
- develop body and gender awareness;
- know when they can and should give their permission and when they should withhold it.

Developing good relationships and respecting the differences between people

The aims are for pupils to:

- develop and experience a range of relationships;
- recognise and understand different types of relationships (QCA/DfEE 2001a).

The framework and guidelines represent considerable progress in re-establishing the importance of personal and social education. However a critical and reflective approach needs to be taken to them and to what is being advocated. Are the values those that a school would want to emphasise? What model of personal and social education is being offered? Is it a limited view of the field? What view of the students and their role in society is contained in the framework? All these are important questions to ask when planning the curriculum.

Sex and relationship education

There is new guidance on sex and relationship education (SRE) from the DfEE (2000a) and this guidance makes reference to the National Healthy School Standard as a supportive framework for the delivery of sex and relationship education. Debates on the guidance centred on the previous emphasis on family values and whether it was acceptable to teach about homosexuality and in what ways. The current guidance proposes that the nature and importance of marriage for family life and bringing up children should be emphasised. There is also an acknowledgement that there are strong and mutually supportive relationships outside of marriage and therefore pupils should learn the significance of marriage and stable relationships as key building blocks of community and society. The guidance also states that the needs of all students should be met within the programme and that obviously includes students who are homosexual.

> It is up to schools to make sure that the needs of all pupils are met in their programme. Young people whatever their developing sexuality need to feel that SRE (sex and relationship education) is relevant to them and sensitive to their needs.
>
> (DfEE 2000a)

This guidance clearly applies to students with learning difficulties.

Sex and relationship education should also start early on – before puberty, sexual attraction and sexual experience. This means that it should be age-appropriate and should link in with the framework for PSHE and contribute to it. The guidance on sex and relationship education at the primary and secondary stages is as follows:

Primary school level sex and relationship education

The curriculum should aim to help students to:

- develop confidence in talking, listening and thinking about feelings and relationships;
- name parts of the body and describe how their bodies work;
- protect themselves and ask for help and support;
- be prepared for puberty.

Secondary school level sex and relationship education

The curriculum should aim to help students to:

- develop positive values and a moral framework that will guide their decisions, judgements and behaviour;
- be aware of their sexuality and understand human sexuality;
- understand the arguments for delaying sexual activity;
- understand the reasons for having protected sex;
- understand the consequences of their actions and behave with responsibility in sexual and pastoral relationships;
- have the confidence and self-esteem to value themselves and others; have respect for individual conscience; and the skills to judge what kind of relationships they want;

- communicate effectively;
- have sufficient information and skills to protect themselves and where they have one, their partner, from unintended or unwanted conceptions and sexually transmitted infections including HIV;
- avoid being exploited or exploiting others;
- avoid being pressured into unwanted or unprotected sex
- access confidential sexual health advice, support and if necessary treatment; and
- know how the law applies to relationships.

The area of sex and relationships education is a very important one for students with learning difficulties because there is ongoing evidence that they are often underprepared for sexual experience or feelings and are at risk too from adults who abuse relationships with young people. There is also the issue of what the adults in these young people's lives expect or allow. It is often difficult to imagine that many young people have the right to a sexual life or sexual experience.

The guidance advocates and good practice shows the importance of partnerships with parents and other adults involved in caring for and educating young people.

The Healthy Schools Standard

There is in the PSHE framework and the Sex and Relationship Guidance considerable cross-referencing to the Healthy Schools Standard and this emphasis on the connections between these initiatives is to be welcomed.

The National Healthy Schools Standard (NHSS) was launched in October 1999. It is jointly managed by the Department of Health and the DfEE. It is based at the Health Education Authority, which is to become the Health Development Agency. Each area has a regional coordinator and there are national criteria for local schemes. Schools will be given the chance to join their local schemes and will be supported in meeting the agreed quality standards. All schools will have the opportunity to join a local scheme by 2002 (DfEE 1999a).

The standards cover the following areas:

- PSHE;
- citizenship;
- drug education, including alcohol and tobacco;
- emotional health and well being, including tackling bullying;
- healthy eating;
- physical activity;
- safety;
- sex and relationship education.

The connections between all three major initiatives here are clear.

Developing ideas about work for people with learning difficulties

Interestingly, Lynda Otten's book about the curriculum for personal and social education for pupils with severe learning difficulties does not deal with the notion of work, careers education and guidance, vocational preparation or work-related learning (Otten 1999). Otten equates the notion of personal and social education with health education. As she states:

Work and work-related learning

> The curriculum (at Piper Hill) was developed with the specific aims of supporting and promoting attitudes, practices and understanding conducive to good health; fostering social skills, self-esteem and a sense of responsibility.
>
> (page 1)

It is understandable that staff writing from the perspective of teachers and nurses in a special school may not have given a great deal of thought or curriculum time over to the notion of work for young people with severe or profound and multiple learning difficulties. Yet this is clearly a notion that has meaning for those young people themselves as they contemplate their options as adults. Our own research conversations with young people with learning difficulties (Byers 1997) have revealed a fascinating range of aspirations for adulthood, some of which are given in Figure 4.1.

> To go back to my special school as a teacher.
> To work in hospitals doing operations.
> To do woodwork.
> To get a job on a building site.
> To work in the woodcrafts section of a sheltered industrial unit.
> To work in an old people's home.
> To be a singer.
> To work in a shop in my home town.
> To be a typist or to work a computer.
> To be a chef.
> To be a stained glass teacher.
> To work on the dustcarts.
> To have a pay day.
> To go to work and have parties.

Figure 4.1 Young people's aspirations for adulthood

These are all real aspirations expressed by real people with learning difficulties. Yet they may elicit a range of responses from the practised professional. Some of these aspirations may seem 'realistic' enough; others may seem to be imbued with a sense of pathos and poignancy. It may touch our hearts, as professionals, to think that our pupils and students may aspire to some of these roles. Some of these aspirations may seem plainly ridiculous and professionals may suggest that these young people need to be helped to come to terms with the unattainable nature of some of these goals.

Perhaps it is this sense of unattainability that keeps Otten and her colleagues from engaging with the question of work for the pupils at Piper Hill. This chapter will propose, however, that it is time to rethink the relationship between learning disability and work. We will undertake this re-evaluation in the context of policy on social inclusion; employment opportunities for people with disabilities; and an awareness of changing realities in the worlds beyond school and college.

There is a long tradition of people with learning difficulties doing work. For example, people with learning difficulties may, in the past, have been seen as useful workers in the family home, undertaking more than their share of household chores as unpaid domestic servants (see, for example, Bessant 1996). People with learning difficulties may still, in some households, have a role in caring for more dependent family members. Frequently, as professionals, we might also extol the virtues of learning to do housework and express this training in domestic skills as an important preparation for life in a group home or hostel. Some of this work may now be seen as bordering on the exploitative. Some of it may be useful and appropriate. It may be important for some people to gain skills in working in the home. What is certain, however, is that all this activity can be characterised as work and all of it is unpaid and devoid of status or prospects.

People with learning difficulties have also worked within placements, for example, in hospitals and other residential institutions. Atkinson and Walmsley (1995) note that, on the day of an inspection in 1943, 87 per cent of the patients at Bromham Hospital (a long-stay mental subnormality hospital) were working. The men were characteristically engaged in farm work (the mental subnormality hospitals of the time frequently achieved self-sufficiency in food while also trading a surplus with other hospitals) or gardening; the women tended to be occupied in cleaning, cooking, sewing or work in the laundry room. At the time, and well into the second half of the last century, long-term work regimes like this were regarded as being dignified, appropriate and even ennobling. It was only as new ideas about therapy, education and development for people with learning difficulties came to fruition in the 1960s and 1970s that this form of work, often entailing long hours and meagre reward, came to be seen as exploitative and unacceptable.

The alternative, proposed in the shape of the community-based Junior and Adult Training Centres and Occupational Therapy Departments within residential provision, was to turn work into a form of therapeutic training. A report of activity in the then newly commissioned Adult Training Centre (ATC) in Luton in 1967 (cited in Atkinson and Walmsley 1995) reveals something about the work regimes that people with learning difficulties experienced, and a great deal about notions of adult status and gender stereotyping at the time. Luton ATC had a carpentry shop where the 'boys' were introduced to tools in order to give them an awareness of danger. The 'girls', meantime, were learning to cook, wash, mend and iron clothes, go shopping and manage a domestic budget. Some ATCs diversified and took on light industrial work on contract from the commercial sector. This enabled some people with learning difficulties (usually those identified as the 'high grades') to move on from scrubbing floors and building bird boxes in order to become occupied in 'sheltered workshops'. These environments sought to simulate industrial production lines and allowed people with learning difficulties to pack, for example, plastocine strips into cellophane wrappers all day, without any prospect of career advancement, for token pay.

Real jobs with real wages?

By the latter part of the 20th century, people with learning difficulties were themselves rejecting these narrow, constrained, exploitative and stereotypical models of work. In 1993, delegates at the International People First Conference in Canada were calling for 'real jobs with real wages'. Those of us who complain about the demands of the workplace might wonder why paid employment seems so important to people with learning difficulties. Griffiths (1994) suggests that work is an important indicator of adult status and that it offers all of us:

- control over our own lives and choices in terms of leisure, lifestyle and activity;
- independence and, in particular, the capacity to run an independent household;
- the possibility of taking responsibility for others;
- finance to support an active social life.

Of course, we all know that work can have its negative aspects, including stress, boredom, ill-health, injury, exhaustion and exploitation. But work may also be perceived as offering all of us a range of potential benefits, including a sense of identity as a 'worker'; enhanced self-image; social status; the dignity afforded to those who 'earn their own way' in life; opportunities to meet people; a structure for each day; and, in the final analysis, something purposeful to do with our time. For people with learning difficulties, according to Griffiths (1994), work may have other important repercussions. People with learning difficulties who work acquire a key indicator of 'normality' that can help them to shed their disabled status. Their self-esteem may be enhanced by a sense of contributing to society rather than constantly being in receipt of benefits, support and special provision. And people with learning difficulties are keenly aware that the productive activity and economic self-sufficiency associated with work are key indicators of adult status (OECD/CERI 1986).

So are 'real jobs with real wages' available for people with learning difficulties? Progression into this form of work certainly began to become a theoretical possibility for people with learning difficulties in the USA during the 1970s. During this time, provision in the States encompassed:

- adult 'day-care' facilities, which were designed to offer pre-vocational and recreational basic skills training for people with severe and profound and multiple learning difficulties;
- 'work activity' programmes, which simulated 'work-like' activity for those unable to work at the pace of the sheltered workshops;
- sheltered workshops, which were supposed to provide time-limited vocational training and workplace evaluation, but which often, in fact, became long-term placements for people engaged in work subcontracted from the industrial sector – renovation, reclaim and recycling work, for example, with some packaging and light manufacturing reminiscent of ATC contract work in the UK.

It is worth noting that all these forms of work entailed low pay, segregation and the ongoing possibility of exploitation. However, provision in the USA also encompassed placements in transitional schemes where people with learning difficulties were said to be preparing for open employment. In theory, people moved on from these schemes into supported employment placements (which we will discuss in detail in subsequent chapters) and some people gained employment in the open, competitive world of work. The underpinning for this continuum of possibilities was a belief in a 'train then place' form of progression in which people with learning difficulties were gradually taught how to work so that they could move on from specialist, sheltered and supported environments towards open employment. In practice, people tended to become stuck on this proposed ladder of development and, again, ended up with narrow options and little prospect of real career progression.

Supported employment

In contrast to this process, in which people with learning difficulties were required to demonstrate work competence before they could gain access to the workplace, the supported employment movement pursues a 'place then train' policy which puts people into jobs then teaches them the skills they need in order to do the work. In the USA, there have been a number of models for supported employment, some of which perpetuate aspects of the separate, segregated, demeaning forms of activity which characterise traditional approaches to work for people with learning difficulties. For example, in the 'work crew' model, a team of workers with learning difficulties might be employed by a commercial organisation and placed under the guidance of a shared 'job trainer' who will go around with them doing peripatetic gardening or cleaning work. In the 'enclave' model, a small group of people with learning difficulties might work within a company, again under the direction of a shared 'job trainer', perhaps supporting particular aspects of an industrial or packaging process. In the 'work bench' model, a small group of people with learning difficulties might be offered systematic training in a discrete task, perhaps assembling particular components within a small business environment.

In any of these models, people with learning difficulties can be said to be engaged in competitive work. They may be based in an integrated setting and, theoretically, have social and occupational contact with non-disabled co-workers on a regular basis. They may also stand to benefit from ongoing training and support opportunities on site. In practice, small groups of people with learning difficulties might tend to spend most of their time working together on separate tasks, rarely coming into contact with other workers. The individual model for supported employment, where an individual is placed in an ordinary work place with on-the-job training and ongoing support from a job trainer, therefore seems to many commentators to offer the best chance of creating access for people with learning difficulties to the benefits of mainstream employment.

More recently, in the UK, we have been able to learn from the American experience. Advocates of supported employment in this country tend to prefer the individual model since it seems to offer more chance of providing real jobs for full pay – 'employment' rather than simply 'work' – with all the social and other benefits that this implies. Successful individual supported employment opportunities for people with learning difficulties could be said to be characterised by a number of factors:

Carefully matched placements

In the most successful supported employment scenarios, there is a high standard of match between the profiles of the worker and the workplace – the right person is placed in the right job. This high degree of compatibility is achieved by thorough profiling of both the worker – their interests, aspirations, previous experience, needs and capabilities – and the workplace – in terms of physical environment and social aspects. Gathering information in order to create honest, accurate and robust profiles requires expertise and experience but can be a crucial factor in the success or otherwise of a placement. Inter-agency collaboration is also important in order to ensure that practical issues (including transport, impact on benefits and any adaptations to the work site) are addressed. Partnership between a range of agencies can also ensure that attention is paid to other, less tangible, factors such as adherence to dress codes, personal hygiene, social behaviour and sustained motivation.

Job site training and advocacy

Experience shows that people with learning difficulties, in order to be successful in employment, need to be trained in job-specific tasks. This training may often be provided in the workplace by a job coach – often a member of staff from the supported employment agency. This approach can successfully impart the skills required, but may serve to emphasise the difference between the new employee with learning difficulties and the rest of the workforce. The preferred approach involves making maximum use of 'natural' systems of support in the workplace. This may involve using other employees as 'mentor' figures, thereby ensuring not only that the new employee learns accurate task-specific skills but also that he or she is connected to the social network of the workplace.

Ongoing support and monitoring

While it is important to ensure that the employee with learning difficulties is supported by the natural social and occupational networks of the workplace, staff from the supported employment agency need to stay in close touch with the developing situation. Ongoing programmes of monitoring and support can enable the supported employment agency to keep lines of communication with company personnel open. The new employee's performance can be maintained under review and retraining or 'top up' training offered as required. It is salutary to note that almost half the people with learning difficulties placed in supported employment may find themselves out of work again after only two years. Vigilance from the staff of supported employment agencies can help to identify and pre-empt problems. A rapid response to emerging problems may make a significant contribution to sustaining placements in open employment for people with learning difficulties. However, supported employment agencies also need to be alert to the fact that jobs in today's commercial environment may be relatively short-lived and that people with learning difficulties, like other employees, will need to be ready to explore new opportunities as the world of work changes.

Follow-up and retention

Staff from supported employment agencies therefore aim to support people in constantly upgrading, refining and extending their work skills. Workers with learning difficulties, like other employees, deserve opportunities for professional development and career enhancement. It is not enough to settle a person with learning difficulties into any job that seems to be sustainable. In the long term, the aim should be to reduce dependence on support, both in the workplace and in life outside, and to help the person with learning difficulties to realise their aspirations in career terms and in terms of lifestyle.

The development of supported employment opportunities has a number of implications for schools and colleges working with young people with learning difficulties. Awareness of these opportunities will have an impact, for example, on curriculum planning and upon transition planning for individuals. Colleagues working in schools and colleges therefore need to ensure that their own professional development encompasses a number of issues.

Firstly, they need to understand the development of supported employment options in terms of both the local and national contexts. Supported employment agencies will have staff who are mandated to work directly with schools and colleges and many will now have early years' workers who will help schools to conceptualise and plan work-related learning back into Key Stages 1 and 2. This sort of early start, located realistically in terms of local options, will be particularly important for future job seekers who have learning difficulties.

Staff in schools and colleges also need to ensure that they teach job-relevant skills, knowledge and understanding to older students through a carefully planned programme of careers education and guidance. This will be partly accomplished by teaching whole cohorts of students about the world of work and integrating work-related learning effectively into the curriculum offer. But individual students should also be provided with a wide range of work experiences to enable them to 'sample' a full spectrum of possibilities for a working future. These experiences should not be limited by teachers' perceptions about work that may offer 'realistic' potential for future employment but should be used to foster a breadth of awareness and a variety of new aspirations in the learner.

Staff in schools and colleges should also develop their capacities to plan and function in direct collaboration with other agencies. These agencies will include local communities and local businesses as well as the statutory and voluntary services for adults with learning disabilities. Staff in schools and colleges supporting transition into employment for young people with learning difficulties should therefore be seeking to make links with colleagues from social services, with health service staff, including therapists, and with representatives of local advocacy groups. The learning mentors and personal advisers of the Connexions service (DfEE 2000c) will be of particular significance where staff in schools and colleges are seeking to develop shared responsibilities in policy and practice.

Of course, professionals will also seek to work in close collaboration with parents, siblings, members of the extended family and other networks of support, including friends and allies in the community. They will also wish to promote choice, autonomy and self-determination by working in close partnership with each young person with learning difficulties. Arguably, while employment should not be seen as the sole defining attribute of adulthood, it should be considered as an important option in the lives of all adults with learning difficulties.

Transition

Full participation

The Association of Supported Employment Agencies is aiming at full participation in employment for all people. The world of employment can be opened up to people with severe and profound and complex learning difficulties in a number of ways.

Schools and colleges can use the formal curriculum and work experience opportunities in order to foster skills and attributes which are valued in the world of work. According to Griffiths (1994), the key attributes of a valued employee include:

- reliability and the capacity to be a conscientious worker;
- motivation and the will to persevere;
- a pleasant and cooperative personality and the ability to make good relationships with other workers;
- the capacity to travel independently;
- high standards of personal presentation, hygiene and social behaviour;
- the ability to understand and follow instructions;
- the capacity to work without constant supervision;
- the ability to problem-solve and initiate solutions;
- the ability to separate work from other aspects of life;
- autonomy and the capacity to survive difficulties and setbacks.

While these attributes may seem to comprise a list of unrealistic objectives for many people with learning difficulties, it is worth noting that the efforts of schools, colleges, families, adult services and communities can be coordinated in order to provide support in many of these areas. It is possible, for example, for families and staff to monitor employees' ongoing compliance with workplace dress codes. Allies in the community, including bus drivers and shopkeepers who encounter people en route to work, can help to promote independent travel.

Employers can, of course, help to open up new opportunities themselves, but they do not need to feel that they are doing this alone. For example, employers may work in partnership with staff from those agencies offering support to people with learning difficulties in order to adapt work-related tasks and develop an appropriate range of job-specific aids and supporting devices. In some workplaces, jigs and work frames, for example, have helped employees with learning difficulties to achieve and sustain task competence. Highly focused techniques, such as the American approach to systematic instruction, can help to train people with learning difficulties in specific tasks. Further, the workplace itself can be adapted to make it accessible to people with learning difficulties and associated physical disabilities. Under the 'access to work' scheme, funding is available to help employers make adaptations of this sort. Some commentators insist that the government should also make money available to compensate employers for lack of productivity in workers with severe and profound disabilities. It is argued that this approach can be cheaper than providing specialist services for these people, notably if there is employment for more than 20 hours per week. Further, many commentators insist that the benefits system needs to be changed in order to enable people with learning difficulties to take greater advantage of the work opportunities that do exist. Benefits and the regulations associated with them can create unhelpful barriers to paid employment; a tendency to settle for part-time solutions; disincentives to find and sustain work; and the pressing fear of a permanent loss of entitlement to benefits.

With the right will, however, employment opportunities for people with learning difficulties can be created. Under certain circumstances, achievable aspects of other people's jobs can be identified and clustered together in new work packages in order to make a job that can be done by a person with a learning difficulty. This sort of 'job carving' may help not only to make the workplace more inclusive, it can also help to release experienced staff from familiar tasks in order to enable them to take on new responsibilities for themselves. It may also be that the aim of full participation in the world of work will only be realised, for those people with the most profound and complex learning difficulties, through the experience of work rather than through full-time jobs. The experience of work should still, however, be gained in real workplaces and it should be experience of real work. In this way, people with profound and complex learning difficulties can benefit from the social interaction that the workplace offers; from the sense of meaningful occupation that work can provide; and from the relationship between occupation and income.

Whole school policy

All the initiatives previously mentioned are promoted as benefiting from a whole-school approach. The Qualifications and Curriculum Authority in its initial guidance on PSHE says that 'a whole-school approach is effective because pupils' personal and social development is influenced by many aspects of school life' (QCA 2000: 6). Reference is made to the self-improvement model of the National Healthy School Standard (DfEE 1999a) which suggests 10 key elements for a whole-school approach:

- leadership, management and managing change;
- policy development;
- curriculum planning and resourcing;
- teaching and learning;
- school culture and environment;
- giving pupils a voice;
- provision of pupils' support services;
- staff professional development, health and welfare;
- partnerships with parents/carers and local communities;
- assessing, recording and reporting pupils' achievements.

And they identify four steps to implementing the framework for PSHE and citizenship:

- developing and implementing a management process for PSHE;
- identifying a governor to take responsibility for PSHE;
- allocating responsibility for teaching PSHE and coordinating staff;
- developing a clear PSHE policy that links with other school policies aimed at promoting pupils' spiritual, moral, social and cultural development.

These lists can be helpful as an aide memoire or a checklist of essential ingredients but they do not ensure that the students' learning is being monitored or reviewed. In March 2000 a group of young people met at the National Children's Bureau and decided to write their own charter for sex and relationship education. It is interesting because it is a very different list and focuses much more on teaching and learning approaches and entitlements.

---

* Every child has the right to sex education in all areas (gay, lesbian, straight, bisexual).
* Every child has the right to express their opinion.
* Every child has the right to specific information, advice, counselling and support.

To achieve this:
* From society we want more openness about sex in general.
* Parents should be able to talk to their children without feeling embarrassed.
* There should be a special sex education team.
* Teachers who feel comfortable to give sex education should be given support.
* Outside visitors should be allowed to come into schools.

We would expect to learn about:
* real-life dilemmas;
* sexuality and relationships;
* peer pressure;
* problems;
* friendships;
* being gay or lesbian;
* contraception;
* STDs;
* HIV;
* pros and cons about sex;
* when is the right time to have sex;
* where to get and get advice [Brook]

We would like sex education to be fun. This would be through:
* role plays and games;
* videos;
* oppportunities to explore dilemmas;
* practising communication;
* discussions that are open and multi-ethnic;
* comments and suggestions boxes allowing pupils to ask questions who would otherwise feel embarrassed and give them a chance to say what they want to know;
* baby dolls;
* outside visitors;
* teenage mothers;
* a gay or lesbian;
* people with different life experiences to express;
* people from clinics.

[NCB 2001]

Figure 4.2 A charter for good sex and relationships education

Many of the issues that are being raised here are ones that will be picked up on in the chapter on teaching and learning. However, the central point that comes from this student charter is that teaching and learning approaches are central in personal and social education.

In the field of personal and social education, monitoring the learning and the quality of it is central to the effectiveness of the curriculum. Research has shown that personal and social education is important and does affect health-related behaviour but that the effectiveness relates directly to the learning and teaching methods (Balding and Bish 1992; Allen 1987; Advisory Council on the Misuse of Drugs 1993). It has also long been known that the personal and social concerns of adolescents and their importance are usually unacknowledged by adults. For example in the past it was common for adults to think that students with learning difficulties did not need to have extensive sex education because this did not apply. More recently it has been matters of mental health that we as adults have found hard to explore.

Effectiveness, impact and reviewing learning

The Mental Health Foundation (1999) has shown that mental health problems among young people are on the increase and that schools have a critical role to play in creating emotionally literate children and in the early identification and referral of children with mental health problems. So there is a need for teachers to find ways of alerting themselves to the genuine concerns of young people if PSE is to be effective. We also know that the timing of PSE provision often lags behind students' concerns and development (Allen 1987). PSE is most effective when it is demanding, responsive and involving, i.e. it needs to address the concerns of students and real-life situations, as argued for in the students charter (NCB 2001). Since the school is often the only site for education or discussion on a range of personal and social issues for children and young people, this last series of points becomes very important (McLaughlin *et al.* 1996).

The other important issue in terms of evaluation and monitoring is that of teacher training and development. As we will see in the next chapter, the range of teaching and learning approaches demanded by effective PSE taxes teacher expertise and development. Many teachers have not received any training, be it initial or in-service, in this area and so feel underprepared for this work. Research has shown that training needs to build confidence and attend to the following aspects (Gysbers 1990; Bolam and Medlock 1985):

- Developing depth approaches to learning. There has been a tendency in the past to focus on a problem-based superficial approach to learning.
- Developing a rationale for the work. Many teachers do not fully understand the purposes of personal and social education.

- Understanding the range of teaching and learning approaches and feeling confident in using them, especially since many of the issues are sensitive or controversial and teachers feel anxious about this.
- Understanding the content.

Finally, the issues of leadership and management of this area of the curriculum are ones that need monitoring. Since this is a whole-school issue and one that addresses personal and social learning in all locations not just the 'courses', it requires considerable skills in managing and monitoring. It is also essential that whoever has responsibility for this work, has the structures and processes to enable them to do the work. They will also require the ability to work with colleagues, senior managers, other professionals and parents or carers.

Part Two: Developing schemes of work

Introduction

We suggest that all members of staff who work with pupils and students with learning difficulties should regard themselves as having at least some responsibility for the personal and social development of those learners. All pupils and students with identified special educational needs are subject to the requirements of the *Code of Practice* (DFE1994). This will frequently mean that they are working towards specific targets focused on aspects of their personal and social development. These targets will represent areas of progress and achievement identified as priorities for them as individual learners (see Chapter 6).

As proposed in the first part of this chapter, pupils and students with learning difficulties also have shared entitlements to learn about issues in relation to their personal and social development which extend beyond these individual targets. We argue here that staff should use all the curriculum-planning structures which apply to other areas of the curriculum in order to meet these entitlements. Some practitioners still tend to rely on established routine and claims about self-evident value in order to establish the contribution that some parts of the teaching day make towards pupils' and students' personal and social development. Break-time, mealtime and changing-room routines may justifiably be seen as an important part of the curriculum for personal and social development, but if these parts of the week are not treated exactly like other teaching and learning opportunities, and subjected to agreed planning, implementation and recording regimes, then staff are failing in their duty to be accountable to pupils, students and parents in this important area of the curriculum. As we have seen, they may also lay themselves open to criticism from external inspectors. This chapter will support the process of bringing these concerns into the same planning framework as the rest of the curriculum.

The curriculum-planning process has been well documented (see, for example, SCAA 1995; SCAA 1996; Byers and Rose 1996). The QCA/DfEE (2001a) *General Guidelines* on planning, teaching and assessing the curriculum for pupils with learning difficulties reinforce and clarify earlier messages. These materials suggest that 'determining a school curriculum' for pupils with learning difficulties entails first establishing aims. Staff who work with pupils and students with learning difficulties can make use of a number of sources in choosing or developing a set of aims for their specific context. As noted above, the National Curriculum (DfEE/QCA 1999a) offers 'two broad aims' which 'provide an essential context within which schools develop their own curriculum'.

Establishing aims

These aims make explicit reference to whole-person development and preparation for adulthood. The QCA/DfEE (2001a) *General Guidelines* build upon these broad aims in proposing that the school curriculum for pupils with learning difficulties might aim to:

- enable pupils to interact and communicate with a wide range of people;
- enable pupils to express preferences, communicate needs, make choices, make decisions and choose options that other people act on and respect;
- promote self-advocacy or the use of a range of systems of supported advocacy;
- prepare pupils for an adult life in which they have the greatest possible degree of autonomy and support them in having relationships with mutual respect and dependence on each other;
- increase pupils awareness and understanding of their environment and of the world;
- encourage pupils to explore, to question and to challenge;
- provide a wide range of learning experiences for pupils in each key stage suitable for their age.

(pages 6 to 7)

These aims make further reference to preparation for adulthood and, arguably, begin to make clear the kinds of confident, competent, questioning, critically aware and autonomous adults that staff, as we have noted in previous chapters, might expect their pupils and students with learning difficulties to become. The QCA/DfEE (2001c) guidelines provide a more specific set of aims for pupils with learning difficulties in relation to the strands in the curriculum for personal, social and health education and citizenship. These aims build on the notions of selfhood (Wall 1977; Hamblin 1978; Watkins 1995) discussed in earlier chapters of this book. For example, the QCA/DfEE guidelines suggest that developing confidence and responsibility and making the most of their abilities relates to pupils' self-concept and self-awareness, self-esteem and self-knowledge and that the curriculum can help pupils with learning difficulties to:

- develop a positive self-image;
- explore, express and communicate their needs, feelings and opinions;
- take responsibility for themselves and their belongings (initially in the classroom, in school, outside school and, later, further afield).

(page 5)

Work on preparing to play an active role as citizens (in Key Stages 1 and 2) and gaining knowledge and understanding about becoming informed citizens (in Key Stages 3 and 4) can help pupils with learning difficulties to:

- make choices;
- take part in group activities and discussions;
- realise that all individuals are important in their own right;
- recognise differences and similarities in people.

(page 5)

Learning about developing a healthy lifestyle across the key stages can enable pupils with learning difficulties to:

- learn about the need for personal hygiene, take part in and maintain personal hygiene routines;
- develop body and gender awareness;
- know when they can and should give their permission and when to withhold their permission, *for example, to communicate 'no'*.

(page 6)

Work focused on developing good relationships and respecting the differences between people can help pupils to:

- develop and experience a range of relationships;
- recognise and understand different types of relationships;

while sex and relationship education should provide the knowledge, skills and understanding pupils with learning difficulties need in order to:

- make informed, positive decisions about their own relationships and lives and about their own safety.

(page 6)

The QCA/DfEE (2001c) guidelines on implementing personal, social and health education and citizenship for pupils with learning difficulties go on to provide further ideas for the 'focus' of teaching in each key stage. The above aims may be sufficient to stimulate debate in most contexts, however, especially since some of the ideas about personhood and an inclusive adult society embedded in these aims may challenge some people's perceptions about what it is to be an adult with learning difficulties. Acknowledging the contribution of OECD/CERI (1986), Griffiths (1994) notes four 'aspects of adult status' which he puts forward as aims for the process of transition from childhood to adulthood for young people with severe learning difficulties:

- *personal autonomy* (full responsibility for one's own life);
- *productive activity* (economic self-sufficiency);
- *social interaction and community participation* (taking an adult role in society);
- *roles within the family* (being a non-dependent son or daughter, a spouse or a parent).

(page 4)

While not all of these characteristics of adulthood are made explicit in the aims listed above (there is little emphasis on economic self-sufficiency in the QCA materials, for example, perhaps because careers education and guidance is not dealt with in its own right), they should inform thinking about personal and social development, as we have noted above. However, Griffiths (1994) asserts that gaining adult status in terms of these characteristics may be problematic for people with learning difficulties for three reasons:

- because their disability 'precludes their achieving the level of competence generally regarded as necessary for adult status';
- because they are not offered 'access to the learning experiences which would enable them to develop greater competence';
- because their rights to exercise their actual or potential competencies are 'not recognised by other people'.

Griffiths proposes that 'parents and professionals' can resolve to minimise the extent to which young people with learning difficulties are 'handicapped' in these three areas. We agree that there are crucial messages here for staff who work with young people with learning difficulties. We suggest, building on Griffiths work, that staff with any form of responsibility for the personal and social development of pupils and students with learning difficulties might adopt a series of aims for themselves and for their work:

- to enable all learners to participate in the full range of learning opportunities;
- to help each learner to gain the widest possible range of skills, knowledge and understanding;

- to provide the means, when required or requested, whereby the limiting effects of specific impairments or disabilities can be overcome, circumvented or minimised;
- to respect the right of young people with learning difficulties, as they grow older, to explore adulthood, to display adult characteristics, to engage in adult behaviours and to gain adult status;
- to negotiate with learners about their choices, preferences, needs, feelings and opinions in relation to all the above.

An example of a set of aims for staff, written up as a 'code of practice' relating to the curriculum for sex education in a school for pupils and students with physical disabilities and learning difficulties, is given in Figure 4.3. This statement brings together many of the themes we have raised in earlier chapters of this book and serves to introduce work which we will discuss in more detail in this chapter.

Determining curriculum entitlements

These aims might help to guide decisions about pupils' and students' entitlements relating to the curriculum for personal and social development. The QCA/DfEE (2001a) guidelines suggest that providing increasing 'breadth of curricular content' in order to extend pupils' access to 'new knowledge and understanding' as they grow older is one way in which staff can promote progression in the curriculum offered through the key stages. We suggest that curriculum entitlements can be determined most effectively by asking why pupils and students with learning difficulties should be denied access to any aspect of the curriculum normally offered to learners in the mainstream of education. The QCA/DfEE (2001a) guidelines certainly propose that pupils with learning difficulties share an entitlement to:

- the full range of subjects of the National Curriculum, including citizenship at Key Stages 3 and 4 from 2002, religious education, sex and relationship education, other aspects of PSHE, and careers education, according to the relevant key stage;
- provision which prepares pupils for adult life, with access to suitably accredited courses as they grow older.

(page 7)

together with 'opportunities to acquire, develop, practice, apply and extend' a range of skills 'relevant to life and learning outside and beyond the school' in a range of contexts across the curriculum (see chapter six). As well as providing for these shared entitlements, staff who work with pupils and students with learning difficulties may need to make additional provision in relation to other important priorities, such as additional personal and social skills, individual support programmes and individual education plans, for pupils and

1. Treat every student as an individual, with dignity and respect.

2. Respect each individual's need for privacy and personal space.

3. Respect the students' need for increased independence as they grow older. Provide frequent opportunities for choice and responsibility to help develop each individual's potential.

4. Take into account the needs and level of each individual student and ensure that methods and resources used are appropriate.

5. Use age-appropriate language and behaviour, for example, young man/woman for older students rather than boy/girl; appropriate dress and personal items, for example, music or books.

6. Use the correct and agreed words for body parts and functions.

7. Be aware of, and celebrate, religious and cultural differences between students.

8. Promote socially acceptable behaviour and means of expression in and out of school.

9. Be aware of the need for separate gender groups in certain situations.

10. Be sensitive to the students' feelings about their bodies. Try not to perpetuate the media myth of the 'perfect body'.

11. Encourage students to be assertive. It is all right to say 'NO'.

12. Don't allow personal feelings or attitudes to dictate responses or impose standards on others.

13. Share and record any concerns.

14. Decisions should be made in a team context. Don't act alone. Seek advice from other professionals where necessary.

15. Refer any complaints or concerns to a senior member of staff or your line manager.

16. Become familiar with the sex education policy and procedures for dealing with situations which may cause concern. (N.B. policies on child protection, behaviour, equal opportunities.)

Figure 4.3 An example of a Code of Practice for staff in relation to the curriculum for sex education

students with learning difficulties. It is for schools to decide how to allocate time to these different elements of the curriculum and we would suggest that it may be appropriate for schools making provision for pupils and students with learning difficulties to allocate significant proportions of time to aspects of personal and social education. The OFSTED (1999) handbook states that personal, social and health education constitutes a 'crucial part of the whole curriculum'. The handbook makes it clear that, in special schools where the quality of the curriculum is very good or excellent, 'high priority is given to pupils' personal development' while the curriculum 'cannot be satisfactory' if it is 'unduly narrow in opportunities for personal development or curricular enrichment'.

The task of agreeing a curriculum profile, showing the time allocated to each of the aspects of the curriculum for each age group, can be usefully informed by undertaking a review or audit of current practice (DES 1989; SCAA 1995). Building on the work of Byers and Rose (1996) and established understandings about the distinctions between continuing work and 'blocked' or discrete units of work (SCAA 1995, 1996), we suggest that an audit of the curriculum in respect of opportunities for personal and social development might be based around the following questions:

- How does personal and social education permeate the life of the school? What opportunities for ongoing personal and social development are presented in the flow of activity throughout the school day?
- How many regular sessions and routine activities are focused on personal and social development in the course of a typical week?
- To what extent are opportunities for personal and social development integrated into regular sessions focused on other aspects of the curriculum?
- How is personal and social development addressed through discrete units or modules of work dedicated to aspects of personal and social education?
- To what extent are opportunities for personal and social development integrated into discrete units or modules of work focused on other aspects of the curriculum?
- How many special events and extra-curricular activities provide opportunities for personal and social development in the course of a school year?

Schools will be familiar with the process of asking questions such as these about timetabled sessions relating to readily defined curriculum subjects. In undertaking an audit of opportunities for personal and social development, however, it is particularly important that full account is taken of:

- unplanned or incidental opportunities in and out of classroom settings;
- personal care routines;
- social and leisure activities;
- occasional events and extra-curricular activities;
- activities outside school;
- links with other subjects.

A form which could be used as a prompt for gathering this sort of information is given in Figure 4.4 In order to clarify the ways in which this audit tool might be used, and to illustrate the sorts of data that might be collected using these questions, an example of a range of possible responses to these questions, drawing ideas from across the key stages and from a range of contexts, is given in Figure 4.5

Since the profile of the curriculum, in terms of breadth and balance across subjects and other aspects, should change as pupils grow older, an audit of this kind would need to be conducted in each age group. The resulting analysis of the use of time in school can be used in order to inform the review of accepted practice and enable school communities to reach informed and considered agreements about the types and quantities of time allocated to personal and social education, expressed as a number of hours per year or a percentage of the teaching week, in each key stage. Information gathered from this kind of audit can also help staff to identify occasions in the teaching week when personal and social development is occurring without the support of policy statements, planning documentation or record keeping or assessment procedures. Experience demonstrates that this is often the case with break times, mealtimes and valuable opportunities for personal and social development which are incidental to or integrated into activities in the school week which are primarily focused on other purposes such as changing before and after sports or swimming. Schools cannot rely on the common-sense or self-evident value of these opportunities in the whole curriculum offer or upon the exceptional memories of staff in recalling and reporting pupils' and students' progress and achievement in hidden corners of the school year. All opportunities for personal and social development are important and should be appropriately documented. Guidance on preparing and maintaining the appropriate kinds of documents follows.

An audit of opportunities for personal and social development in key stages
Opportunities for personal and social development that permeate the life of the school
Regular sessions and routine activities focused on personal and social development
Opportunities for personal and social development integrated into regular sessions focused on other aspects of the curriculum
Discrete units or modules of work dedicated to aspects of personal and social education
Opportunities for personal and social development integrated into discrete units or modules of work focused on other aspects of the curriculum
Special events and extra-curricular activities providing opportunities for personal and social development

Figure 4.4 Blank audit proforma

An audit of opportunities for personal and social development across key stages

Opportunities for personal and social development that permeate the life of the school

For example: making choices and decisions; communicating preferences; asserting views and perspectives; working with staff or other pupils or students; solving problems independently in learning situations; recording progress; reviewing achievements.

Regular sessions and routine activities focused on personal and social development

For example: mealtimes; snack and drink breaks; play and leisure time; use of the toilet and other personal care routines; arrival at school and in new classrooms; rotas for school or classroom responsibilities; Circle Time; celebrating work in assembly; tutorials.

Opportunities for personal and social development integrated into regular sessions focused on other aspects of the curriculum

For example: changing at the beginning and end of PE, swimming or games lessons; keeping fit through sports and games; health and safety issues in food technology sessions; relaxation to music or in a multi-sensory environment.

Discrete units or modules of work dedicated to aspects of personal and social education

For example: units of work focusing on awareness of self and others; body awareness; personal care; aspects of health and safety; emotions; gender; childhood; puberty; adulthood; ageing; sex education; the world of work; work experience.

Opportunities for personal and social development integrated into discrete units or modules of work focused on other aspects of the curriculum

For example: discussing motivations and dilemmas in story time; learning about aspects of human biology in science; sharing aspirations in careers guidance sessions; learning about moral issues in RE; exploring feelings and emotional responses in drama sessions.

Special events and extra-curricular activities providing opportunities for personal and social development

For example: charity fund raising events in the local community; elections to the school council; a scheme for cleaning up part of the local environment; visits to work places; visits to other schools for sports or performing arts events.

Figure 4.5 Audit proforma with examples

Making policy

The audit process described above can help school and college communities to make or review policy. Building on the work of Sebba (1995) and SCAA (1996), we would argue that schools should set out their intentions for pupils' and students' personal and social development in a brief policy statement which covers:

- a definition of the subject area – what is personal and social development and what are the broad aims and objectives of the curriculum for personal and social education?
- a rationale for including this work in the curriculum offer, taking account of the contribution it makes to providing breadth, balance and relevance across the whole curriculum – why try to promote personal and social development through teaching and learning?
- a review of links and contributions to other subjects, skills, themes, aspects and dimensions in the whole curriculum – what role does personal and social development play in relation to the rest of the curriculum offer?
- a record of posts of responsibility for this area of the curriculum – who is the coordinator for personal and social development? Who teaches and supports this area of the curriculum?

Guidelines for teaching

The audit process can also begin to support the development of guidelines for implementation (SCAA 1996). These guidelines may be far more detailed than the brief policy statement described above and may build into a handbook or dossier supporting teaching and learning in each area of the curriculum. In this case, the guidelines would help to answer the question: how is personal and social education taught in this setting? Guidelines for promoting personal and social development for pupils and students with learning difficulties may therefore provide:

- statements about pedagogy, giving some sense of the teaching methods that are appropriate and the learning demands that are therefore implied for pupils and students – how is personal and social development taught and how do pupils and students learn?
- a description of the various systems that are in place for planning within and across class and age groupings (including year groups and key stages) – how is teaching and learning in relation to personal and social development planned for pupils and students at various ages and in various groupings?
- guidance on contexts for implementation – where is personal and social education taught in the various age groupings? What rooms or teaching spaces are appropriate and/or available? In which settings should pupils' and students' personal and social development be pursued?

- lists of resources – what aids, equipment and materials are available and/or appropriate in order to support pupils' and students' personal and social development in the range of age groupings and settings for teaching and learning?
- a discussion of access issues and differentiation strategies – how can the curriculum for personal and social education be interpreted, adapted, extended and modified in order to promote access, engagement, participation, progress and achievement for pupils and students who experience difficulties in learning?
- guidance on monitoring, recording, assessing and reporting progress and achievement – how should personal and social development for pupils and students with learning difficulties be recognised, noted, celebrated and accredited?
- notes about inter-agency team work – how are other professionals (including subject specialists, support staff, therapists, social workers, advisory teachers and educational psychologists) involved in promoting pupils' and students' personal and social development?
- information about staff development opportunities – how can colleagues enhance and extend their own expertise in promoting personal and social development?
- information about curriculum plans and ongoing curriculum development processes – what schemes of work for personal and social education exist? What is the agreed programme for monitoring, evaluating, reviewing and revising the curriculum for personal and social education? What is the agenda and time scale for further development of the curriculum for personal and social education? Who is responsible for coordinating these developments?

An extract from a set of guidelines for teaching is given as Figure 4.6. In this case, the guidelines were written by staff working in a school for pupils and students with profound and multiple learning difficulties. Colleagues in this school wanted to support one another in undertaking intimate care procedures in ways that would:

- protect staff and pupils and students;
- ensure that pupils and students were respected as private individuals;
- value this aspect of the work of the school as part of the whole curriculum for personal and social development.

The guidelines were based on some of the advice given in Downs and Craft (1997a).

Intimate care is defined as any care of a personal nature which a student requires.

The purpose of these guidelines is:

a) to protect pupils and staff;

b) to ensure that this aspect of our provision is valued and that high standards are maintained;

c) to provide guidelines on procedures or issues relating to this area.

Staff should also be familiar with school policies and guidelines for child protection, sex education and behaviour.

1. Intimate care should ideally be carried out by someone who has a positive and long-term relationship with the student. New staff should be accompanied when getting involved in intimate care tasks. There should be continuity of intimate care provided by the same carers. There should also be consistency of care, with the same approach provided both in school and at home or in the residential setting.

2. Intimate care tasks are not an interruption to the daily timetable, but must be valued as an important part of the school curriculum. They provide opportunities to develop independence and age appropriate skills, increase dignity and raise self-esteem for the students.

3. Intimate care must take place within as private an environment as possible. If more than one member of staff has to be available to provide intimate care, then staff will try to provide care in as dignified a manner as possible. This involves explaining to the student what is happening; seeking their consent for procedures; and being aware of one's own approach to conversation throughout the intimate care activities.

4. Any intimate care tasks of a particularly difficult or unusual nature should be discussed with others involved in the student's care, so that the dignity of the student is maintained and the uncertainty for the carer is reduced. A record of some sort is required to ensure that information may be shared, for example, with new staff, and reviewed.

5. Intimate care tasks should not be attempted unless the carer feels confident and sure how to proceed. If in doubt, ask a colleague.

6. If a member of staff is concerned that during the intimate care of a student she/he:

Figure 4.6 An example of guidelines for staff – intimate care procedures in a residential school for pupils with physical disabilities and learning difficulties

- accidentally hurts the student;

- the student seems sore or unusually tender in the genital area;

- the student appears to be sexually aroused by his or her actions;

- the student misunderstands or misinterprets something;

- the student has a very emotional reaction without apparent cause.

Any such incidents should be reported as soon as possible to another person in the team and a brief written note made of it.

7. As a general guideline, the correct clinical terms should be used for private parts of the body.

8. The environment should be pleasant, clean, hygienic and relaxing. Appropriate resources should be readily available.

9. Intimate care should also be provided in a physically safe environment. Staff should be aware of lifting and handling guidelines and there should be adequate circulation space within the bathroom area. Appropriate resources should be available.

10. It can be particularly difficult to provide intimate care in community settings and maintain the same standards of privacy and dignity. Staff should plan ahead, being aware of the location and layout of toilets, take spare clothing, and ensure that staff of the same sex accompany students, if possible. Staff should carry identity cards bearing the school name, address and phone number and explaining that this member of staff is responding to the needs of the student she/he is with.

11. If staff members become aware that students are mis-using intimate care situations, then all those involved need to discuss the issues and decide on appropriate procedures.

12. Students with disabilities have sexual feelings and it is possible that both males and females could become sexually aroused during intimate care procedures. Individual procedures will need to be discussed by all those involved in the care of the student. As a general guideline, physical contact should not be given whilst someone is sexually aroused. Carers should also be aware of their language and maintain student's dignity.

13. All carers must be aware of the potential for abuse, particularly when dealing with aspects of intimate care. All staff should have received child protection training and should be aware of the availability of child protection guidelines.

Figure 4.6 (Continued)

Creating a long-term

According to the guidance provided by QCA/DfEE (2001a); SCAA (1995 and 1996); and Byers and Rose (1996), long-term planning can be used in order to:

- show the relationship between continuing work and discrete units or modules of work;
- note the amounts of time to be devoted to each unit of work;
- define the content and coverage of units of work in terms of programmes of study, key stages and the age groups of pupils and students;
- show aims in terms of the knowledge, skills, concepts and attitudes to be promoted;
- indicate links between subjects or opportunities to run units in parallel;
- plan for progression from year to year; across key stages; and through transition from one age band to another.

Schools will be familiar with the process of planning in the long term for subjects in the curriculum. We suggest that the same processes should be applied to various aspects of personal and social development and to the content of the curriculum for personal, social and health education and citizenship (DfEE/QCA 1999a; QCA/DfEE 2001c).

The extract given in Figure 4.7 is taken from a long-term plan for personal and social development in a school for pupils and students with physical disabilities and profound and multiple learning difficulties. It shows a range of units of work focusing on sex and relationships education for students in the school's post-16 unit (see also Downs and Craft 1997b; Johns *et al.* 1997. Further detail, taken from the medium-term plans for this programme of work, is provided below.

Medium-term plans

If long-term plans are used to ensure smooth and steady progression in curriculum content across year groups, key stages and age bands, medium-term plans can be used in order to outline the subject matter to be addressed during a term or half-a-term. Medium-term plans should build upon and conform to the information given in long-term plans, refer to those long-term plans and take the framework for teaching and learning established in long-term plans into a more substantial level of description. Good-quality medium-term plans should therefore:

- clearly define the objectives for learning to be shared by pupils or students in a particular time frame for teaching (usually a term or half-a-term);
- exemplify key activities for typical groups of pupils or students at each age stage, often showing how activities follow one another and build on previous teaching and learning in sequence;

1. Working with Others	2. Self-Awareness and Self-Esteem	3. Personal Hygiene
Year 1 • Establishing routines • Group building (new group) • Roles and responsibilities • Awareness of self and others • Cooperation and team work	• Appearance • Likes and dislikes • Abilities and interests • Gender • Making choices and decisions • My disability	• Exploring products • Male and female products • Choices and preferences • Retail outlets • Changes in our bodies and the need for hygiene
5. Body Awareness	**6. Keeping Healthy**	**7. Relationships**
Year 2 • Parts of the body • Male and female bodies • Similarities and differences • Changes in our bodies • Pregnancy • Inside my body • Public and private	• Nutrition – a balanced diet • Body changes (weight gain and loss) • Similarities and differences • 'Fitness' and 'relaxation' – activities for health and comfort • 'Fitness' at home • Community resources for health and fitness	• Family • Friends • People around me • Other people's relationships • Directing others • Independence • Roles • Advocacy • Thinking of others • Social opportunities • The wider community • Leaving school

Figure 4.7 An extract from a long-term plan for personal, social and health education in a post-16 unit for students with profound and multiple learning difficulties

• outline the differentiation strategies and teaching methods which can be used during a unit of work in order to promote access and participation through a variety of learning styles;
• list the resources, environments and items of equipment which are available or which are appropriate for use during the unit of work;
• define the likely range of outcomes towards which pupils and students might work and which might represent opportunities to assess progress and achievement.

As with other aspects of the curriculum, time devoted to the development of high-quality medium-term plans for personal, social and health education and citizenship will reduce the time staff need to spend on a day-to-day, week-to-week basis doing short-term planning. In effect, working from thorough long- and medium-term plans can free staff up to concentrate on teaching and learning and pupils' and students' personal and social development.

An example of medium-term planning, relating to the long-term plan given as Figure 4.7, is provided as Figure 4.8. This medium-term plan was drawn up for students with physical disabilities and profound and multiple learning difficulties and addresses self-awareness and self-esteem. The material covered in this unit draws upon the pioneering work of authors like Downs and Craft (1997b); Johns *et al.* (1997).

The medium-term plan given as Figure 4.8 includes notes about opportunities for recognising progress, assessment and accreditation. There are now many forms of accreditation that support schools and colleges in validating and celebrating the achievements of their pupils and students with learning difficulties. Some of these systems focus on aspects of personal and social development (for example, ASDAN, ALL). The development of Records of Achievement and Progress Files has also helped staff to provide appropriate means of accreditation for pupils and students with learning difficulties. Some schools (see, for example, Caviglioli 1997; and Reynolds and Caviglioli 1999) have devised their own accreditation procedures based on achievements in relation to the key skills. One of the practitioners we consulted in preparing this book, however, argues that the availability of 'specialist' accreditation, while it is clearly helpful for many pupils and students, does not necessarily, in public terms, provide 'parity of esteem for significant achievement'. He argues that staff should never underestimate the capacities of students with learning difficulties to gain accreditation within mainstream systems. He reports the achievements of one young man with additional chromosomes/Down syndrome, working in an inclusive setting in a London borough, who attained seven GCSEs in addition to his Gold ASDAN Youth Award and a Welsh Board Certificate of Education for communication skills. Clearly not all these qualifications accredit aspects of personal and social development, but there is a clear sense in which recognition of achievement on this scale in the public arena would contribute significantly to self-esteem.

Planning in the short term

As we have indicated above, we contend that good long- and medium-term curriculum plans can reduce the need for formal short-term planning. In our experience, session-by-session lesson planning can become a repetitive and bureaucratic burden upon experienced staff. The QCA/DfEE (2001a) guidelines state that:

> good-quality, medium-term curriculum plans, the short-term targets set in pupils' IEPs and the management plans detailed in individual support programmes will provide most of the information that staff need in order to prepare short-term plans for teaching.
>
> (page 18)

Unit title: self-awareness and self-esteem

The following areas are covered in this unit:

- Appearance
- Likes and dislikes
- Abilities and interests
- Gender
- Making choices and decisions
- My disability

Objectives:

During this unit, we intend students to learn to:

- recognise and participate in familiar routines;
- show interest in their own appearance;
- show interest in the appearance of others;
- recognise changes made to the appearance of self or others;
- express preferences for particular items of clothing or toiletries;
- show interest in new or unfamiliar environments;
- show awareness of their own strengths or achievements;
- indicate preferred activities or stimuli;
- show awareness of male/female differences;
- show awareness of their own gender;
- show awareness of their own disability and others with disabilities.

Activities

The following suggestions represent examples of the kinds of activities and experiences that could be offered during this unit:

1. Appearance
Activities which encourage students to look at themselves and consider aspects of their appearance. Examples might include:
- looking at self in mirrors, in photos, on video; hearing voices on tape;
- looking at others' appearance: similarities and differences;
- close face-to-face work, for example, feeling facial features;
- changing appearance through clothes, make up, hats, masks, face paints etc;

Figure 4.8 A medium-term plan addressing aspects of personal, social and health education in a post-sixteen unit for students with profound and multiple learning difficulties.

- hair and facial 'beauty' treatments;
- fashion and image;
- visits to shopping centres to look at clothes, toiletries, mirrors, etc;
- famous people and 'image'.

2. Likes and Dislikes
Activities which focus on individual likes and dislikes and comparisons with others. Focus on how students express likes and dislikes. Record responses and preferences.

3. Abilities and Interests
As above with an emphasis on the strengths of individual students. Sharing and celebrating strengths and achievements.

4. Gender
Activities to encourage awareness of students' own gender/sexuality. Examples include:
- single sex groups;
- male/female differences (for example, a man shaving);
- listening to music/voices;
- items associated with males/females;
- clothing/toiletries;
- visits, for example, to department stores.

5. Making Choices and Decisions
Encourage students to assert themselves by making choices about aspects of their daily lives. Activities to encourage control and direction of others using individual means of communicating. Encourage staff to be responsive to students needs/wishes.

6. My Disability
Encourage awareness of own disability and feelings about disability. Offer positive images of disabled people. Offer awareness of constraints imposed by society, for example, access issues. Encourage control through IT and the need to respect individual means of communicating.

Outcomes:

Progress and achievement may be demonstrated when a student:

- shows recognition/anticipation of a routine activity and joins in appropriately (for example, responds to or identifies signifier, greets others on cue);

Figure 4.8 (Continued)

- shows recognition of own image in:
  a) mirror
  b) photo
  c) video
  d) other
- looks towards adult or peer and responds to appearance;
- shows interest in image of another in photo or picture;
- responds to change made to:
  a) own appearance
  b) other's appearance
- expresses like/dislike of particular items of clothing/toiletries;
- recognises own clothing or toiletries;
- shows interest in new or unfamiliar environment (for example, head up, and looking round);
- responds to praise or celebration of own achievements;
- expresses preference for particular activities or stimuli;
- responds to features of males or females (for example, voice, facial hair);
- identifies:
  a) own gender
  b) another's gender
- identifies with others with disabilities;
- identifies features of environment which:
  a) help access
  b) hinder access

Context for Learning

At school with opportunities for some activities to take place at the bungalow and in the wider community, for example, visits to department stores.

Resources

Resources required include:
- students own clothes and wash bags;
- mirrors;
- cameras;
- video and TV;
- toiletries;
- magazines;
- male and female voices on tape (spoken or sung);
- staff of both genders
- activities/stimuli known to be enjoyed by students.

Figure 4.8 (Continued)

Accreditation

Opportunities for accreditation through ALL (evidence required): Core skills.

Personal Skills	Module 2	Demonstrate own strengths
	Module 4	Recognise familiar people
Communication	Module 2	Attend and respond in a 1:1 interaction
	Module 3	Attend and respond in a group
	Module 4	Show recognition of self
	Module 5	Indicate needs and preferences
Numeracy	Module 1	Recognise routine events
	Module 4	Recognise differences in measurements
	Module 5	Recognise pictorial/symbolic information
I T	Module 3	Make a graphic record
	Module 4	Use a TV
	Module 5	Use an audio-visual record
Home management	Module 2	Use shops
	Module 4	Look after own clothes and belongings
Community	Module 1	Explore a variety of community facilities

Figure 4.8 (Continued)

Staff will need to share information about their immediate intentions for teaching and learning with colleagues and with pupils and students themselves and this may be achieved most efficiently through paperwork. Staff teaching new units of work or working with new pupils and students for the first time may also wish to map out their short-term plans carefully on paper. Some staff may prefer, for their own purposes, to maintain fairly detailed teaching logs. In our view, however, short-term planning may frequently be an ephemeral and largely internal process which does not need to be rigidified in formal documentation.

This does not mean that short-term planning is unimportant, simply that it may be informal. We would suggest that short-term planning has a number of important functions, for example, it can help staff to:

- plan activities in detail – session by session, week by week – for specific groups of pupils/students;
- relate teaching methods to individual learning styles;
- consider pupil/student groupings;
- differentiate for particular pupils/students;
- deploy staff and equipment;
- integrate individual pupil/student targets (set in terms of key skills) into group activity;
- plan opportunities to record and assess in relation to:
  - curricular objectives;
  - performance criteria related to accreditation;
  - individual pupil/student targets.

The development of appropriate approaches to teaching, as an element in short-term planning, can be a key factor in promoting personal and social development. In the following chapter, we discuss the impact that different teaching methods, engaging pupils and students in a range of learning styles, can have upon learners personally and socially.

Monitoring, evaluation and review

Monitoring, evaluation and review procedures should be seen as a key part of the curriculum planning process. Documentation should enable staff to:

- record evaluative comments about long-, medium- and short-term plans which will contribute to the review of curriculum plans and policy;
- monitor the effectiveness of the teaching methods, differentiation strategies and resources used;
- monitor the responses of individual pupils and students in order to prepare for the review of objectives in schemes of work and targets in IEPs;

- record the progress made by individual pupils and students in relation to the objectives in schemes of work and the targets in IEPs;
- prepare to celebrate and accredit significant achievements.

Pupils' and students' personal and social development will be enhanced if they are actively involved in all the processes listed above. We return to these issues in Chapter Six.

Chapter 5

Learning and teaching for personal and social development

This chapter will explore the processes of learning in the field of personal–social development and the implications for teaching. There will be a review of recent approaches to learning and teaching in the field of students with learning difficulties and of personal and social education. The central argument will be that these two trends merge and that the moves towards more involvement of students in their own learning and the active model of learning advocated in the personal and social field are all part of the same approach.

Introduction

> Learning is personal and social and is enhanced by personal–social attention.
>
> (Watkins 1995)

Reference was made earlier to the work of Vygotsky (Faulkner *et al.* 1998) who is an example of the learning theorists who have shown that to separate out the cognitive and socio-cultural aspects of learning is to make a false separation. Research into schools by Rutter has also reinforced this point:

Learning and personal and social education

> In years gone by educationalists have debated whether either a task-orientated, nose-to-the grindstone approach or an emotionally supportive approach designed to make children want to be at school and enjoy their learning was better. The choice is artificial and misleading. Both aspects are necessary for optimal learning.
>
> (Rutter 1991)

Enhancing the personal and social aspects of learning has been shown to enhance achievement. Slavin's work (1990) has shown the power of cooperative learning approaches. There is currently an understanding that personal and social qualities, such as perseverance and resilience, are central to learning in school and to lifelong learning (Claxton 1999). As Watkins (1999) and others have shown, the pace of knowledge growth and information generation is so huge that schools cannot hope to keep up, but students can be prepared to have the dispositions to carry on learning and many of these are attitudinal. Perkins (1995) has characterised these dispositions as being ready, being willing and being able. The need to take an interest; persist with difficulty; express an idea or opinion; take responsibility; and get involved are all key to learning, and they are largely the personal and social elements of learning.

In this context *the focus* of the learning is also personal and social. It is the learning about self and the world. There are strong connections to action in this arena. For example much personal and social education focuses on behaviour and interaction – drugs education, sex education and citizenship are just three of the arenas. We know that here the model of active learning is the most appropriate. Figure 5.1 shows this model.

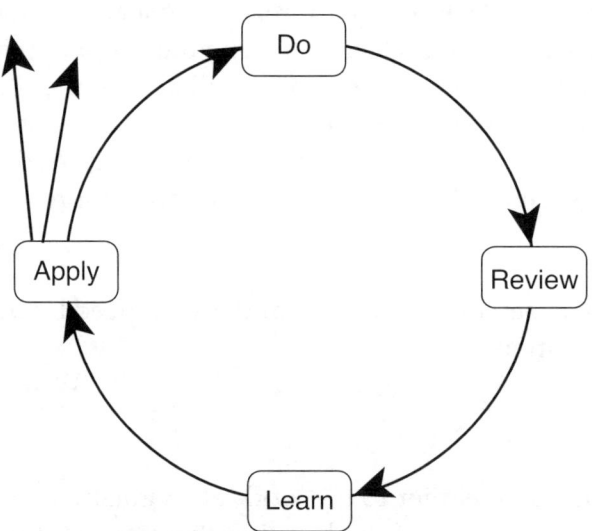

Figure 5.1 The Model of Action Learning

This model reflects also many of the processes of personal–social learning in young people. First they do something, then they get feedback of some sort and on the basis of that they review the strategy and plan the next action. These cycles are the ones described by Dewey *et al.* (Kolb 1984) when discussing experiential learning. The 'Do' phase of the learning is the planned learning activity. It might be reading something, looking at something, doing a collaborative exercise, a simulation or it might be an activity outside the classroom. The 'Review' element is where there is reflection and review on what was learned. This process needs to be structured and sequenced. Here is where the points are drawn out through discussion or reflection. The 'Learn' phase is where the learning is drawn out and future learning is identified. The 'Apply' phase is where the transfer of learning takes place. Here students need to apply what they have learned to other contexts and to plan the action or set goals. Transferring learning from one context to another is one of the most difficult processes to achieve and one of the areas that requires a lot of attention in teaching. In Chapter Four reference was made to the students charter for sex education (NCB 2001). This charter reinforces many of these points. The students argue for active learning methods and for an engagement in the lessons and the curriculum.

The use of a greater range of teaching methods, many based more on a model of experiential or action learning, is something that has occurred in special schools and in work with students who have learning difficulties. Collis and Lacey (1996) and Babbage *et al.* (1999) outline how teachers in special schools have adopted different models of learning at different times. In the 1970s the predominant model was the objectives approach. In this model learning was largely individual; precise and measurable; behaviourally quantifiable; tightly controlled; according to rigorous success criteria; and step by step. This approach was heavily reliant on behaviourist principles. Then came a more active emphasis. Nind and Hewett (1994), for example, developed Intensive Interaction, which promotes active control for learners in the context of highly responsive relationships with staff facilitators. Collis and Lacey (1996) and Ware (1996) show how multi-sensory and contingency-sensitive environments can be used to make learning more interactive for pupils and students with learning difficulties. The High/Scope approach provides a further example of active learning principles in practice. The approach has three main phases, being plan–do–review. The similarities between this and the action learning model are evident. Babbage *et al.* argue (1999) that the National Curriculum and the introduction of Records of Achievement helped to extend the range of teaching and learning strategies being used in special schools and to develop complementary relationships between the two contrasting models outlines above.

Approaches to teaching and learning for students with learning difficulties

We can conclude that there is now some agreement that the methods used in special schools and in personal and social education need to be varied and that the model of action learning is particularly appropriate for personal–social learning. It needs to be relevant, continuous and build on previous and known learning. Evidence shows that in personal and social education there has been a tendency to focus on factual information or on fear or problem-based approaches and these have been ineffective. For example a recent OFSTED report on drug education in schools makes a very familiar point:

Principles for learning and teaching approaches in personal and social education

> In the majority of lessons which feature drug education pupils achieve adequate levels of knowledge and understanding of drugs and their effects. Some lessons are too short for effective learning to take place: in particular, pupils do not have sufficient opportunity to develop appropriate skills or to reflect on their attitudes towards drugs.
>
> (OFSTED 2000)

So too much attention has been given to the knowledge component and not enough to the skills or attitudinal aspects.

The need to start where students are and to involve them is also stressed in previous guidance on PSE and citizenship, 'Pupils' own experiences provide the starting point in education for citizenship. Curriculum provision should build on personal experiences and encourage pupils to see citizenship as something which extends beyond their immediate experiences and relationships' (NCC 1990b).

The current notion of active citizenship builds on the active learning approach. The learning needs to be based in the world of the student and it involves action. If students are to learn from their own experience and to struggle with what that means then teachers will have to allow a certain amount of risk. Letting students be responsible for their own learning means that teachers have to allow students to struggle. It also means giving real responsibility to the students so that they can really struggle. Winup (1994) shows how school and class councils can be used in this way.

Action is very important in skills learning and the opportunities to try out approaches in a safe setting is key. This is strategic learning too. Students need opportunities to experiment with strategies for handling situations such as how to say no to a difficult or undesirable request. So thus far we have said that learning needs to be:

- based on the action learning cycle;
- continuous;
- relevant;
- starting from where the student is and building on previous experience and knowledge;
- starting small;
- helping students to make meaning and transfer learning from the learning activity;
- focusing on knowledge, skills and attitudes;
- giving students responsibility and support;
- encouraging learning dispositions such as resourcefulness, resilience and reflectiveness (Claxton 1999).

Taking the group seriously

The other key characteristic of social learning is that it takes place in a group context and the group is very powerful in shaping the context. There has been much talk of the power of the peer group and recently in education we have taken this seriously enough to begin to harness the power of the peer group for educational ends. Peer mentoring, peer counselling, peer mediation and peer tutoring are all phrases and processes found in many schools now (see Cowie and Sharp 1996 for more on this).

The charge could well be laid against both mainstream and special schools that in personal and social education the group has not been taken seriously enough. One of the side-effects of the objectives model described earlier is that little work was done in groups and individual work was over-emphasised. If students have communication difficulties it is tempting not to work in groups.

Watkins (1995) makes a strong and succinct case for why the group should be taken seriously in PSE and citizenship. He argues that groups offer:

- more efficient arrangements for the teacher;
- increased communication and engagement about a learning task;
- a range of ideas and perspectives.

Also that groups demand:

- the use of communication skills;
- collaboration on some occasions or some tasks;
- groups processes when faced with problems to solve;
- skills of identifying and making decisions.

Groups may:

- recognise and enhance social processes which support learning;
- become supportive places, including for learning;
- be used to simulate social processes which occur elsewhere;
- provide a platform for preparing for other group experiences, outside the group in the future etc.;
- provide a context for reflecting on our own performance;
- provide opportunities for people to give and receive personal feedback;
- become safe contexts for supporting growth and experimentation.

The notion of learning to work with others is not widespread in classrooms. The skills and processes outlined above are complex and ones that adults struggle with. Just as we design learning and teaching opportunities to learn about other aspects of the curriculum, so should we design a curriculum for learning about groups and for developing our ability to work in groups. A curriculum of this sort would include such elements as:

- learning how to adopt and reflect upon the different tasks and roles in a group;
- learning about the different stages of group development and how to contribute to the group at each stage. The framework of *forming, norming, storming, performing and ending* (Tuckman 1965) is now quite a well-accepted one;
- learning how to collaborate and reflect on the nature of the collaboration;
- developing an awareness of group processes and group communication;
- learning how to manage conflict and disagreement in a group.

This is one of the most underdeveloped and necessary aspects of teaching and learning in personal and social education. Texts such as Stanford and Stoate (1990) can help those who wish to explore this further. As Rose (1991) and Byers and Rose (1996) argue, good groups are built, they do not just happen. The process needs to be conscious and explicit and it takes time.

Sensitive and controversial issues

We have discussed how central values are to the field of personal and social education and also how values education is a core aspect of the curriculum. In personal and social education and citizenship education we are dealing with both sensitive and controversial issues. This has frightened many teachers because back in the late 1970s and early 1980s this became a highly political issue and debates about matters such as the guidance on sex education have been heated. Many have attempted to take the controversy out of the curriculum but the territory is still full of controversial and sensitive issues. Unfortunately in response to fears about being political and to scare stories in the press about teacher behaviour in sex education classes, many teachers have adopted a strategy of not talking about such issues. This is because teachers feel underprepared for the situations they encounter and the matter of teacher development will be discussed later in this chapter.

We can define a controversial issue as one where there is disagreement about values and beliefs and where there is emotion or passion. A sensitive issue is where there may be a general consensus about an issue but the private or personal nature of it makes it sensitive. As already stated the tendency has been in the recent past for teachers to retreat from this territory due to the heated debates about it. This is intellectually and morally dishonest but it is also something worth taking a stand for since, in not talking about something, there is a condoning of that position. Staff will be engaging in controversial and sensitive issues. Some useful principles when working in this territory are given by Bridges (1986) and include:

- a respect for persons including the right to hold different views;
- a concern to cultivate the personal autonomy of young people;
- an honest acknowledgement of the true state and status of opinion;
- a readiness on behalf of teachers to detach from their opinions as far as is possible;
- a concern to teach the reasons, evidence and argument underlying that opinion;
- a concern to teach the controversy and not just one person's view of the proper conclusion of the controversy;
- a concern to cultivate a constant alertness and ruthless criticism of those beliefs which we take most for granted.

The sensitive aspects of PSE and citizenship are connected to teacher development and the use of a wide range of learning and teaching approaches. Teachers are often under-confident because they have not had the chance to explore the issues in a safe environment conducive to reflection and exploration. The sensitivity of many issues is related to their personal nature although they may also be controversial. Using methods that are indirect such as third-person case studies and story telling are some of the ways in which we can respect the sensitivity of students and teachers. Other people have developed the use of puppets and other dramatic and active learning methods. The organisation *Image in Action* have specifically focused on developing materials and activities for students with learning disabilities and have produced a useful text – *Let's Do It* (Johns *et al.* 1997) – for those who wish to have detailed guidance on approaches in sex education (see Chapter Four). Their work has shown that drama-based methods work well with students with learning difficulties because they enable them to engage in a direct way with the issues without being hindered by lack of language.

The whole area of teacher development and in-service education is a very important one for all the evaluation evidence in this field shows that many teachers have received none or very little initial or in-service education in this area (cf. Bolam and Medlock 1985; and HMI 1979). The teaching and learning methods are demanding and particularly those related to working with groups and active learning. Many of the methods are challenging and threatening for teachers, for example role play. Teachers need support in developing and reflecting on their learning and teaching approaches. Teachers were most lacking in an understanding of the aims and purposes of personal and social education and a framework for personal and social development. So in-service work is a priority area here.

Teacher development and PSE

These are areas of learning where there is feeling and controversy. The issue of the affective dimensions of learning are very important here. Babbage *et al.* (1999) advocate learning profiles as a way of taking into account learner preferences and feelings around learning. They argue that a continuum of feelings could be used to reflect on how students felt about particular learning approaches and topics. The continuum uses the following headings:

Ease   Comfort   Neutrality   Challenge   Frustration   Stress

These are useful headings to reflect on how students respond. Claxton (1999) argues that we need to think about the comfort zone that students have and what is it in the learning environment that will contribute to that and how we can take students in to the growth zone in a constructive way.

Babbage *et al.* (1999) also provide a set of prompts which can be used to enable pupils and students to review their own learning and to develop a sense of themselves as learners. The practice of involving pupils and students in the detail of teaching and learning processes is an aspect of personal and social development to which we return in the final chapter of this book.

Chapter 6

Personal and social development – the individual dimension

Introduction

This chapter explores the process of promoting personal and social development with individual pupils and students who experience learning difficulties. We argue that, in practice, individual education plans (IEPs) are frequently over-burdened with targets that are already written into schemes of work and over-complex. They may address issues that are tangential to key areas of learning for an individual or be occupied with long-term management protocols. What is more, they may propose ways of working which run counter to the values of inclusive practice and active participation for learners.

We therefore explore guidance on the development of IEPs and note the ways in which they can be focused on areas of personal and social development identified as priorities at annual review. These areas may include some of the key skills and other priorities for learning identified by QCA/DfEE (2001b). We discuss the use of individual support programmes in the development of ongoing management strategies and contrast these protocols with a sharply focused approach to the setting and review of targets in IEPs. This chapter closes with a discussion of partnerships in the IEP process. These approaches will foster pupil involvement at all stages and help staff to take account of the views and perspectives of families and friends. Interestingly, these participants will often bring to meetings a clear focus on issues in personal and social development.

Guidance on the development of individual education plans (IEPs)

The original *Code of Practice* (DFE 1994) did not offer practitioners a great deal of guidance on the development of individual education plans (IEPs). The *Code* suggested that an IEP should set out:

- the nature of a pupil's difficulties in learning;
- the special educational provision to be made in response to those difficulties, with details of staffing arrangements and any resources needed in order to implement specific programmes;
- targets for action, with specified dates for achievement;

- notes about parental involvement and the involvement of other agencies in addressing a pupil's pastoral or medical needs;
- arrangements for monitoring, assessment and review.

The *Code* also noted that IEPs should not lead to separate teaching. Staff were encouraged to implement IEPs 'in the normal classroom setting' where possible, although it was also acknowledged that some IEPs would require a 'co-ordinated cross-curricular and inter-disciplinary approach' if they were to address a pupil's special educational needs effectively.

Within a year of the publication of the original *Code* (DFE 1994), it was apparent to many commentators that an IEP could not be used as a whole-curriculum cure-all. Ramjhun (1995), for example, described any attempt to use the IEP as a means of addressing all of a pupil's difficulties as a 'pointless exercise'. He suggested instead that IEPs should focus on 'one or two areas of difficulty' considered to be the 'priority' areas for action. Ramjhun (1995) argued that 'the intention of the IEP is to concentrate on the priority problem'. Piling up the language of focus and specificity, he emphasised 'the need to be selective and specific' if this 'focussed, concentrated approach' is to be effective.

SCAA (1996) offered some guidance about the priority areas on which IEPs might focus for pupils with profound and multiple learning difficulties:

> The priorities identified from pupils' individual needs may relate to any aspect of the whole curriculum. The priorities identified for pupils with profound and multiple learning difficulties will often relate to the skills of communication, information technology or to personal and social development.
>
> (page 15)

In emphasising the notion that IEPs should address whole-curriculum issues, SCAA suggested that the subjects of the curriculum are properly addressed via curriculum plans and schemes of work. Treated in this way, the subjects may provide a 'teaching context' (SCAA 1996) in which individual priorities may be meaningfully pursued. However, IEPs themselves would not necessarily focus on matters drawn from the programmes of study for the subjects of the National Curriculum. SCAA's alternative proposition, that IEPs might often appropriately focus on key skills and personal and social development, was reinforced by OFSTED. The Chief Inspector of Schools (OFSTED 1998), for example, suggested that IEPs should contain clear targets, including those relating to 'behaviour and social development', in order to help schools to strike 'a balance between brevity and detail' in pupils' IEPs.

DfEE (1998) followed this up, stating that IEPs are 'important for children at stages 2 and 3 of the *Code* or with statements', thereby clarifying the notion that staff should support all pupils experiencing significant special educational needs, including those learning in special schools with the support of statements of special educational need, through the development and implementation of IEPs. However, according to the DfEE (1998):

> … some schools use IEP formats that are unnecessarily elaborate. There is a risk of these being paper exercises, less useful than they should be for busy teachers. IEPs are generally most helpful when they are crisply written, focusing on three or four short-term targets for the child, typically relating to key skills such as communication, literacy, numeracy, behaviour and social skills.
>
> (Chapter 2; para 6)

DfEE has reinforced this message in subsequent guidance and has stated that the revised *Code* would 'provide more guidance on IEPs' (DfEE 1999c). The draft version of the revised *Code* (DfEE 2000b) follows all the principles noted above and emphasises that the IEP should record only that which is additional to or different from the differentiated curriculum provision, which is in place as part of provision for all pupils. The QCA/DfEE (2001a) *General Guidelines* on planning, teaching and assessing the curriculum for pupils with learning difficulties reinforce these recommendations, emphasising that IEPs should set out strategies 'over and above' the differentiated approach to the school curriculum and should focus on 'three or four individual targets in key areas'.

Individual support programmes

IEPs should, however, focus on learning and, we suggest, should not contain lengthy sets of instructions about ongoing programmes of support. QCA/DfEE (2001a) recommend the use of individual support programmes, annexed to the IEP, which set out management procedures and protocols and offer staff guidance about issues like:

- the consistent use of mobility or communication aids;
- the management of medical or paramedical issues, such as drug regimes or epilepsy;
- the use of specialised lighting or positioning equipment in order to maximise access to learning for pupils and students with sensory or physical impairments;
- the regular use of therapeutic or quasi-therapeutic interventions, such as hydrotherapy or Intensive Interaction (Nind and Hewett 1994);
- the provision of individual counselling and guidance sessions (McLaughlin *et al.* 1996);
- the management of difficult behaviours and emotional responses (see below);
- the provision of support for personal care routines, such as eating, drinking or using the toilet, and intimate aspects of pupils' and students' personal lives, including maintaining personal hygiene.

Menstruation

As Rena has now started her periods it is important that we are prepared and able to help her deal with them as well as possible. The following have been suggested as guidelines:

- Record the dates she starts and finishes her periods so that we can anticipate when her periods are due and monitor how long they last.
- Be aware that she may be tearful, upset, have mood swings or experience an increase in epileptic seizures leading up to her periods.
- When she starts her periods, ensure she has her 'toiletry bag' containing:

  sanitary towels
  fresh wipes
  body spray

This bag should only be used just at this time to remind her and her helpers that she has her period and that extra care should be taken over her hygiene.

- Change pads as often as is reasonable, using wipes and sprays to maintain freshness.
- A daily bath – this is essential, at a time most suitable for her, for example, after returning from school and/or in the morning.
- During her periods offer paracetamol (2 tablets – up to four times a day if needed but particularly before bed) if she seems uncomfortable or tearful.
- Offer a warm milky drink at night.
- A warm water bottle wrapped in a towel on her tummy may be comforting.
- Generally give her extra care and attention and make her feel special.

Figure 6.1 An example of an individual support programme for a student with physical disabilities and learning difficulties

We give two examples of individual support programmes which address key issues in personal and social development as Figures 6.1 and 6.2. The names of the pupils and students have been changed in order to protect their anonymity. One support programme was developed in order to support Rena with the onset of menstruation. The other programme shows how staff negotiated a protocol for allowing Tom private time in which to explore his sexuality. Both these students have physical disabilities in addition to learning difficulties and live in a specialist residential setting.

Masturbation

Mrs Petty has raised with residential bungalow staff the issue of allowing Tom some private time in order to explore his body and/or masturbate. In order to do this Tom's nappy should be removed or loosened. At present, Tom has private time when he is using his pot, but may be restricted by the shape of his pot or his sitting position. At home Tom is given a choice before his bath of whether he goes straight into the bath or if he would like to be left alone for a short time in a safe position. The bathroom areas and bathing routine at the bungalow do not appear to allow for this, so the following strategies were put forward at a recent meeting in order to address the issue when Tom is at school:

1. Find out how Tom makes this choice at home. What sign does Mrs Petty use? Is there evidence that Tom understands what it means?
2. Use this sign to teach Tom a symbol which he could use to make the choice at school.
3. The symbol used could be 'private' accompanied by 'time' and 'bed'.
4. This choice to be offered in Tom's bedroom before his evening bath.
5. Tom should then be given time alone on his bed.
6. All staff should be aware that this is Tom's 'private' time. Tom should be able to see someone putting the 'private' sign on the door.
7. Allow Tom 20 minutes on his bed. If he appears to need more time (for example, if he has an erection) leave him for more time.
8. Explain to Tom that it is time for his bath.

Additional issues/future work

- Need to ensure that Tom is comfortable with the situation and that he understands the choice.
- If Tom appears upset or bored when left ask him if he would like to do something else.
- It will not be appropriate to include this symbol option in Tom's standard communication book. He will need a separate wallet. We need to discuss the alternatives which will be presented, for example, 'private time' 'bedtime' 'bath' or 'T.V.'
- Discuss further sex education work with Mr and Mrs Petty. What further work do they feel Tom is ready for? Discuss teaching materials, for example, male and female body parts; information about intercourse/masturbation using symbols/drawings, dolls.
- Ensure that all staff are comfortable with this strategy before proceeding and that they are fully aware of the procedures and of the school's policies re-intimate care and child protection.
- Discuss how we monitor the effectiveness of the strategy, how this is recorded and where we go next.

Figure 6.2 An example of an individual support programme for a student with physical disabilities and learning difficulties

In summary, where staff need to set out a programme of intervention, support or management which will remain in place for some time and which does not include short-term targets for learning, we recommend the use of an individual support programme. An IEP should be developed where staff, in close association with a pupil or student and his/her family, wish to set a small number of targets focused on priority areas of learning for an individual pupil or student.

We have already noted that IEPs should not simply repeat skills, knowledge and understanding addressed in differentiated schemes of work. Where staff try to make IEPs cover material across the range of subjects, they can become overloaded and unresponsive. We propose that each pupil's IEP should reflect the focus of the statement of special educational need and address key priority targets for each individual learner which go beyond the differentiation of shared experiences in the curriculum. Used in this way, the IEP can become an efficient and sharply focused tool for monitoring progress in relation to the statement and as a means of gathering evidence towards the re-evaluation of the statement's relevance on an annual basis.

Developing priority targets in IEPs

The key skills

Where IEPs do focus on key priority targets for individual learners, they can be an important vehicle for promoting personal and social development. The key skills, set out in the National Curriculum (DfEE/QCA 1999a) and further elaborated in *Developing Skills* (QCA/DfEE 2001b), provide one set of contexts in which this can be achieved. The six skill areas which are embedded in the subjects of the National Curriculum and which are described as key skills are:

- communication;
- application of number;
- information technology;
- working with others;
- improving own learning and performance;
- problem solving.

Each of these categories of key skills may, at one time or another, constitute a priority area of learning for an individual pupil with learning difficulties and may therefore be used as a focus for a target in an IEP. For example, we suggest that learning to communicate, beyond the parameters of the differentiated curriculum for English which will be addressed through schemes of work for reading, writing and speaking and listening, will be likely to be a priority for many, if not all pupils with learning difficulties through most of their school career. Learning to communicate, as a cross-curricular and extra-curricular key skill, may also make a very significant contribution to pupils' and students' personal and social development. Some of the illustrations given by QCA/DfEE make this very clear. The *Developing Skills* booklet (QCA/DfEE 2001b) describes the key skill of communication as encompassing, for example:

- responding to others;
- interacting with others;
- recognising and obtaining information;
- communicating for a variety of purposes (for example, expressing feelings or forming and maintaining relationships);
- communicating appropriately in different contexts (for example, local shops, the workplace and the home).

The examples which illustrate the use and application of information and communication technology also show how this key skill can make a contribution to pupils' personal and social development. QCA/DfEE (2001b) suggest that information technology skills can be used, for some learners, in promoting independence; for enabling and improving communication; and as a source of information.

The other key skills may also, at various times in their lives, constitute important priorities in the personal and social development of individual pupils and students with learning difficulties. In emphasising that IEPs can appropriately address pupils' personal and social development, Tilstone *et al.* (2000) give examples of targets which focus on pupils improving their own learning and performance. Tilstone *et al.* suggest that it is disappointing to note that relatively few IEPs address the important process of learning how to learn. The QCA/DfEE (2001b) guidance on *Developing Skills* helps to redress this situation by proposing that thinking skills, or 'knowing how to learn', may mean, for some pupils and students with learning difficulties, developing sensory awareness and perception in any and all of the senses or gaining early thinking skills, including the capacity to predict, anticipate and remember.

Other priorities

QCA/DfEE (2001b) suggest that there are other skill areas which may often be regarded as constituting priorities for learning for some pupils with learning difficulties. These 'additional priorities' include:

- physical orientation and mobility skills;
- organisation and study skills;
- daily living skills;
- leisure and recreation skills;
- personal and social skills.

We will now look in more depth at what some of these priority areas of learning may entail and how these areas can be used in order to promote pupils' personal and social development through IEPs. Physical orientation and mobility skills may constitute important priorities for some pupils and students with physical disabilities in addition to their learning difficulties. In so far as these skills may help learners to develop independence, they may be considered to have an important role to play in personal and social development. Similarly, organisation and study skills, while not directly related to personal and social development, may help young people with learning difficulties to manage their own time effectively, at work and at leisure; to sustain interest and motivation; to complete tasks; and to take responsibility for activities and outcomes.

Daily living skills, community skills and leisure and recreation skills

Daily living skills are, as QCA/DfEE (2001b) note, 'about practical preparation for adult life'. They include domestic skills such as:

> * making drinks and snacks;
> * preparation of food, cooking and home management;
> * the ability to plan for a balanced diet;
> * following instructions and recipes;
> * cooking skills, for example, slicing, grating, whisking, chopping, mixing, pouring;
> * using appliances, for example, kettle, toaster, microwave, cooker, food processor;
> * understanding health and safety in the kitchen, for example, hygiene, safe behaviour and actions.
>
> (page 17)

And community skills such as:

> * developing a social sight vocabulary;
> * using different facilities and amenities in the community, for example, cafés, park, leisure centres, playground, library, public toilets;
> * getting to know a local area;
> * developing shopping skills, for example, locating the shop and items in it, the use of lists, checkout procedures;
> * using a telephone;
> * getting help, for example, from police, community nurse, doctor;
> * the practical use of money;
> * planning for and using public transport.
>
> (pages 17 to 18)

QCA/DfEE (2001b) give leisure and recreation skills as a separate area and note that these skills are relevant across all age groups. Leisure and recreation skills may include:

> * communicating preferences and choices, for example, choosing between two familiar activities in school, choosing a game for the group in a club session, choosing from a wide range of local leisure activities;
> * making effective use of unsupervised time, for example, break time, lunch time, time at home;
> * becoming involved in social organisations, for example, Scouts, sports club, youth organisations;
> * using external amenities in local areas, for example, swimming pools, ten-pin bowling alleys, cinemas;
> * choosing, watching, listening to and evaluating media, such as radio and television.
>
> (page 18)

Clearly, many of these skills will be taught to groups of learners through regular domestic and social routines; in timetabled sessions focusing on these important aspects of personal and social education (see Chapter Four); and through schemes of work addressing aspects of the curriculum, including the core subjects, careers education and design and technology. However, these are also skills which may need to be addressed as additional priorities in IEPs for some pupils and students at certain stages in their school careers. For this reason, we reproduce here the illustrative examples given by QCA/DfEE without attempting to generate an exhaustive checklist. Individual members of staff, working in partnership with other professionals, families and the learners themselves according to the mandate provided by the annual review process, will be best placed to break these areas down into finely tuned and individualised targets for particular pupils and students.

Personal and social skills, behaviour and managing emotions

Significantly for this book, QCA/DfEE also give illustrative exemplification of personal and social skills as a further additional priority area. Noting that these skills have strong links with the curriculum for personal, social and health education, QCA/DfEE (2001b) break personal and social skills down into three sub-divisions: personal care skills; managing their own behaviour; and managing their own emotions. QCA/DfEE suggest that personal care skills include:

- dressing and undressing;
- eating and drinking;
- personal hygiene;
- using the toilet;
- medical routines.

(page 15)

Again, many of these areas of learning will be addressed through timetabled sessions; regular routines and activities through the school or college day; and during preparation for other sessions (changing before and after sports or swimming sessions, for example). Where appropriate, however, carefully focused personal care targets set in IEPs can help individual pupils and students with learning difficulties to achieve independence in these important areas of their lives. Where learners remain dependent upon adults for support in attending to their basic needs throughout their school or college careers, staff must make sure that they have 'as much control as possible' (QCA/DfEE 2001b) over these personal care and daily living activities. IEP targets can help to promote that control.

According to QCA/DfEE (2001b), pupils and students with learning difficulties are 'no more and no less likely to engage in behaviour that challenges' than other learners of the same age. Staff need to be aware that, for some learners who experience difficulties in communicating their preferences and needs in other ways, unusual behaviour may represent attempts to communicate or interact. These unusual behaviours may include:

- self-injurious behaviour;
- confrontational non-compliance;
- extreme states of avoidance and withdrawal, often associated with obsessive and ritualistic behaviours;
- avoiding tasks, behaviour which disrupts, being easily distracted or especially active or hyperactive;
- aggressively inappropriate sexual behaviour.

(page 15)

Some learners' behaviour will be so severe and so persistent that it will need to be addressed through a formally constituted behaviour management plan. This kind of plan may be built into an individual support programme (QCA/DfEE 2001a) for a particular pupil or student. Behaviour management plans can call upon a number of different traditions in responding to behaviour that challenges (see, for example, Ayers *et al.* 1995). Targets that help pupils and students to 'recognise, manage and moderate their own behaviour' (QCA/DfEE 2001b) can be included in IEPs in order to promote self-management or, at least, shared control over difficult behaviours.

Jelly *et al.* (2000) give examples of the sorts of negotiated IEP targets that can help to promote behavioural self-responsibility among pupils with special educational needs.

Like other learners, pupils and students with learning difficulties may also need support in learning to manage their own emotions. QCA/DfEE (2001b) suggest that this may be particularly true when learners:

- experience change in their personal circumstances at home and at school;
- are coping with frustration and failure;
- are managing responses to new or difficult situations;
- express extreme positive or negative reactions to other people;
- are learning to live with loss, grief and bereavement;
- are adjusting to adolescence and adulthood;
- are experiencing low self-esteem.

(page 16)

There are group strategies, such as the use of nurture groups (Bennathan and Boxall 2000) or circle time (Mosley 1996) which can help young people learn to recognise, come to terms with and manage their own emotions. Time for strategies like these can be set aside in curriculum plans and timetables. Individual strategies, including the provision of tutorials, counselling and guidance sessions set out in individual support programmes (see above) and targets set in IEPs, can also be used where the self-management of emotional responses becomes a particular priority for an individual learner.

Setting and reviewing targets

In Figure 6.3 we provide a selection of targets drawn from real IEPs for pupils and students experiencing a range of learning difficulties. We offer these here in order to emphasise the ways in which IEP targets can, and should, address key skills and other priorities for learning which focus on aspects of personal and social development. More detail about these processes and the ways in which they can be developed in whole-school policies, practices and systems for record keeping, accreditation and target setting can be found in Caviglioli (1997) and Reynolds and Caviglioli (1999).

- To build positive relationships with peers.
- To include other children in play activities.
- To gain an adult's attention to indicate:
  - he wants an activity to be repeated:
  - he wants an object.
- To sign for 'more'.
- To learn to undo buttons independently.
- To work at a given task for two minutes.
- To bring the appropriate equipment to lessons.
- To stop at the kerb and look for traffic.
- To shop for two self-specified items independently.
- To develop confidence in speaking to wider groups of people.
- To work with a partner on practical tasks.
- To team up with Lee and go to college on our own.

Figure 6.3 Examples of IEP targets focused on aspects of personal and social development

We are not suggesting that each IEP should contain targets in relation to all the skill areas noted above. However, priorities for learning for individual pupils and students with learning difficulties may be identified in these sorts of areas, in discussion between parents, pupils and professionals from a range of agencies, at annual review. The annual review meeting may then be used in order to identify a wide-ranging set of aims for the year ahead. This set of aims may encompass a variety of areas of work which are additional to and different from the matters to be covered in schemes of work for the year ahead and may include progress which could be achieved at home and out in the community as well as in school.

The annual review meeting may then be used to identify a first set of priority IEP targets for the weeks ahead. These targets, in line with the guidance summarised above, will be few in number (between three and six); will focus on those aims discussed at the annual review meeting which seem to address the most pressing priorities in the pupil's life at the time (possibly relating to personal and social development); and will be designed to be achieved in a matter of weeks (aspiring to achievement in half-a-term but perhaps expecting targets to be achieved within a term).

Staff should meet regularly with the pupil or student (and perhaps parents too) in order to monitor progress towards IEP targets. Targets should be reviewed as and when they are achieved, but there should be regular opportunities (once a term in many schools; more frequently in some settings) built into the tutorial programme for the review of the whole IEP. At this regular tutorial or interim review meeting, each target should be considered in turn. The checklist of questions given in Figure 6.4 may help staff and pupils to work through some useful discussions in relation to each target in the IEP. These questions emphasise the process of

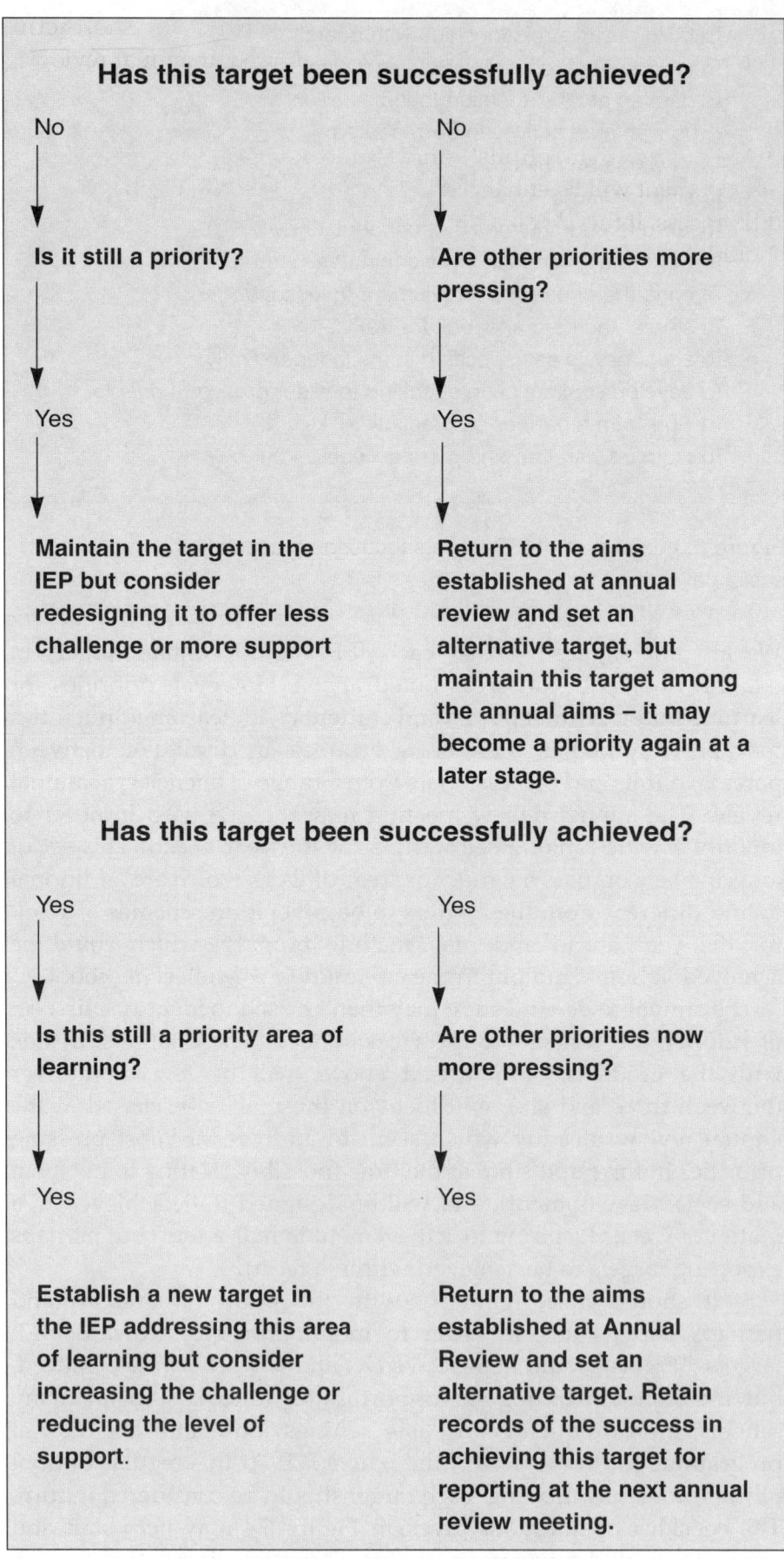

Has this target been successfully achieved?

No   No

Is it still a priority?   **Are other priorities more pressing?**

Yes   Yes

Maintain the target in the IEP but consider redesigning it to offer less challenge or more support   **Return to the aims established at annual review and set an alternative target, but maintain this target among the annual aims – it may become a priority again at a later stage.**

Has this target been successfully achieved?

Yes   Yes

Is this still a priority area of learning?   **Are other priorities now more pressing?**

Yes   Yes

Establish a new target in the IEP addressing this area of learning but consider increasing the challenge or reducing the level of support.   **Return to the aims established at Annual Review and set an alternative target. Retain records of the success in achieving this target for reporting at the next annual review meeting.**

Figure 6.4 Questions to support the review of targets in IEPs

maintaining a focus on a small set of priorities for short-term learning selected from a range of aims identified at annual review.

We propose that pupils' and students' personal and social development will be enhanced if they are involved at all stages of the IEP process. If this involvement is to be meaningful, then information should be in a form which is accessible to learners and which motivates and enables them to take an active role in setting targets, reviewing their own progress and recording their own successes and difficulties. Lawson (1998) gives a range of examples of strategies for involving pupils, including the use of symbols (Detheridge and Detheridge 1997) and pictures. Figures 6.5 and 6.6 illustrate some of the ways in which pupils and students can be enabled to become involved in target-setting and record-keeping processes. Those pupils with emerging or established literacy skills can obviously be given access to more conventional target-setting or recording sheets.

Pupils should be seen as partners in working towards goals in IEPs. This will help to promote self-esteem and confidence as well as helping to ensure that pupils own their targets and are motivated to work towards them. This may mean using local advocacy services (Tyne 1994) or making sure that each pupil has a designated member of staff with whom he or she can discuss difficulties or concerns. For pupils with profound and multiple learning difficulties, the assessment of subtle affective responses may be highly significant in trying to ascertain pupils' views about their educational experiences. Coupe O'Kane and Goldbart (1998) offer important guidance on these aspects of practice and Ware (1996) has alerted staff to the key role they have in enabling pupils with the most profound difficulties to achieve some sense of control over their environment. Nind and Hewett's (1994) work has also enabled staff to explore ways of entering into meaningful negotiations with learners who have complex aggregations of difficulties with learning, communication and social interaction. Nind and Hewett's more recent work (see, for example, Nind and Hewett 1998) has indicated that Intensive Interaction can also be used to help people with autism to become involved in useful dialogue with staff and caregivers. Approaches like this stand in some contrast to the highly structured, heavily directive approaches which are more commonly proposed for use with people with autism and which, in many senses, stand in opposition to the negotiated approach to learning proposed in this chapter.

For those pupils who have the benefit of verbal communication, there are many aspects of 'talking cures' which might prove helpful – solution-focused brief therapy, for example, emphasises the notion that the learner must set his or her own goals for development and this approach has been used with some success with pupils experiencing emotional and behavioural difficulties (Scott-Bauman 1996). This approach was also characteristic of some of the work described in Jelly *et al.* (2000).

Involving pupils in the IEP process

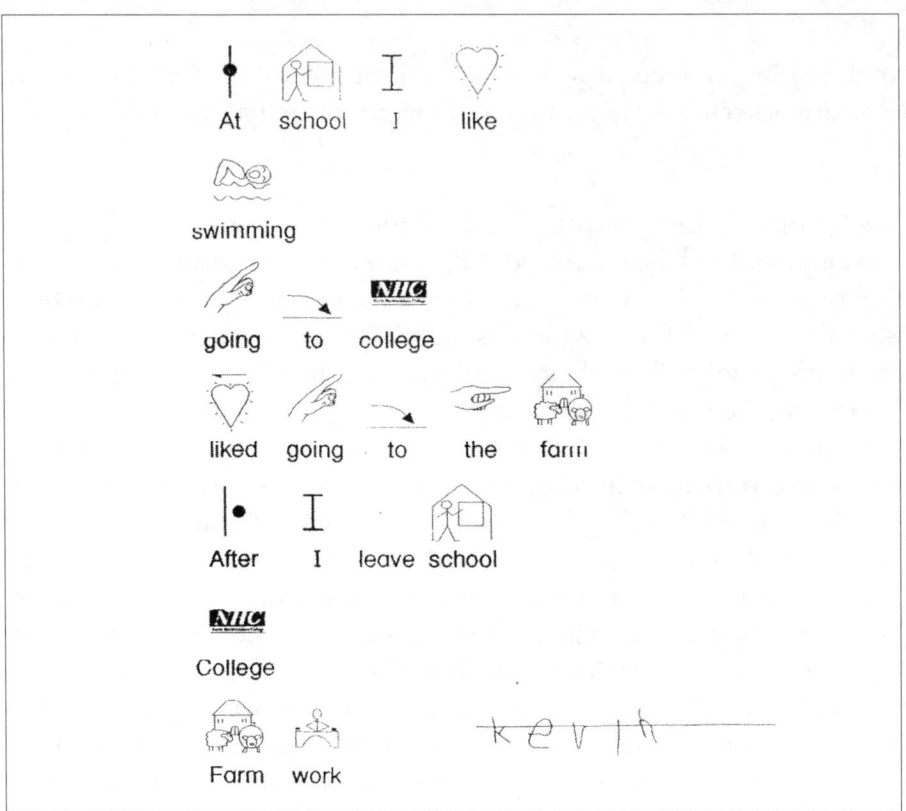

Figure 6.5

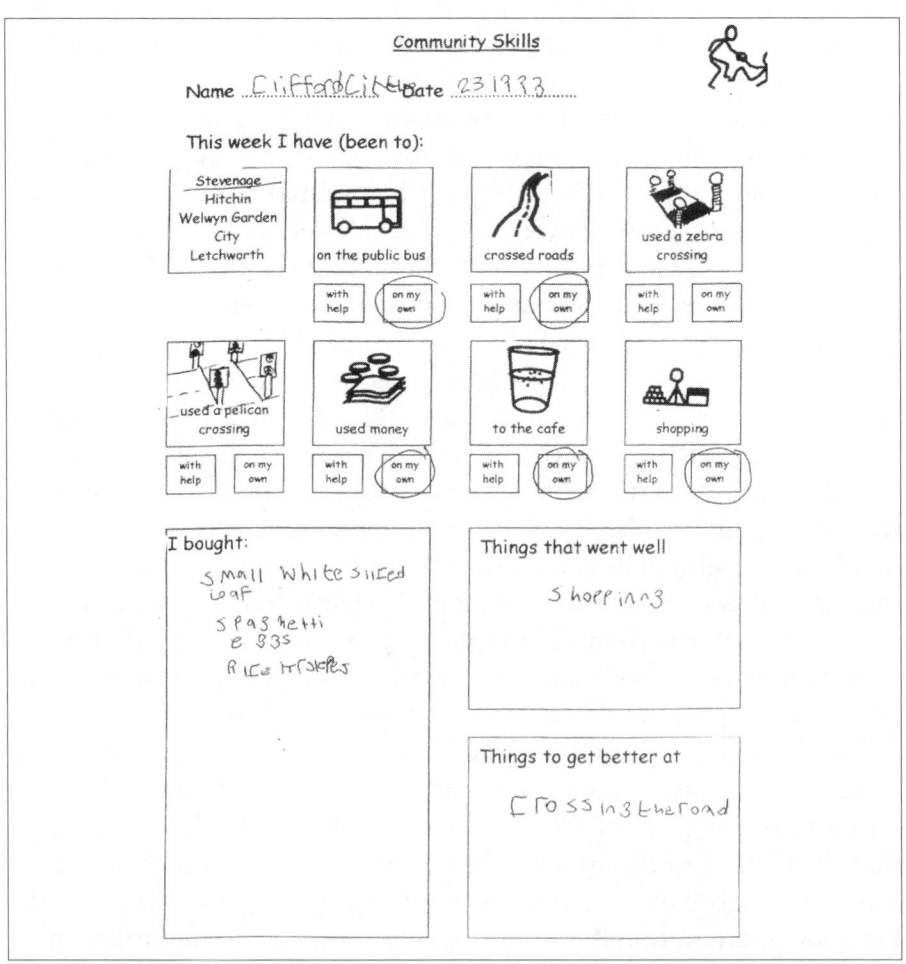

Figure 6.6

The involvement of young people and their families in various aspects of the IEP and annual review processes can also be enhanced by an awareness of person-centred planning procedures. These are becoming more commonly used in adult services and are having an impact on work in schools and colleges. The phrase 'person-centred planning' is used to describe a 'family' of planning styles (Sanderson 1998) which are focused on working with individual people, their families, friends and supporters in order to address two key questions:

- Who are you and who are we in your life?
- What can we do together to improve the quality of your life now and in the future?

Involving families in the IEP process

The various approaches to person-centred planning share a number of common principles.

People should be involved in developing the plans which affect them. Staff can help to make this happen for an individual with learning difficulties by:

- involving the person in documenting their own narratives, stories and histories;
- discovering and recording preferences with the person;
- just spending time together;
- talking to people who know the person; asking questions about the whole range of the person's life experience; and listening to a wide range of answers, comments and perspectives;
- being prepared to join with the person, and family members and friends, in speculating, fantasising or 'dreaming' about new possibilities and aspirations for the future.

We have heard of examples of a wide range of media being used to document people's personal histories, including photographs, video and collections of real objects used as prompts for memories of significant events. We note that Coupe O'Kane and Goldbart's work (1998) provides powerful ways of discovering and recording preferences for people with whom staff experience the most profound difficulties in communication. We acknowledge that many 'dreams' and aspirations expressed by people with learning difficulties may not seem, to professionals, to be attainable. We suggest that they may be very important, however, in helping to shape small steps towards goals and to inform decisions which move in positive directions towards ideal states.

People should be involved in planning meetings. Staff can help to make this happen for an individual with learning difficulties by:

- working to make any meeting as accessible as possible;
- constantly striving to work 'with' the person;

- being responsive to the messages that the person may be seeking to communicate, learning to 'listen' and to 'hear' in the person's preferred style of communication;
- communicating clearly and effectively, again taking account of the person's preferred communication style;
- reflecting, with other participants in the meeting, on the extent to which involvement is achieved and can be improved;
- offering the person time and support in order to help him or her to prepare for the meeting;
- enabling the person to decide who attends and to choose the time and venue of the meeting;
- giving people a central, active role in the meeting itself;
- focusing the meeting on positive achievements, progress towards goals and ways to realise dreams, needs and wishes.

Ware (1996) and Nind and Hewett (1994) offer helpful work on learning to listen, to hear and to respond to people who communicate in unconventional ways. Fergusson (1994) provides an overview of techniques which can be used to develop a multi-modal, multi-dimensional environment for communication. We have also heard of multi-modal profiling techniques, involving information and communication technology, being used to enable individuals with learning difficulties to be in control of the collation and presentation of summaries of their own achievements in review meetings. This may entail, for example, loading video clips, still images, scanned paperwork and a sound track into a Power Point presentation which can be initiated and controlled, during a meeting, by a single switch.

People should be involved in monitoring the plan. Staff can help to make this happen for an individual with learning difficulties by:

- negotiating and establishing agreements or contracts between the person and service providers;
- making direct payments available to the individual person;
- facilitating a person-centred planning process which is independent of services.

The idea of agreements or contracts for teaching and learning is becoming familiar to staff who work in educational settings. Much of the more recent work on disaffection and self-management of behaviour (see, for example, Jones and Charlton 1996) has emphasised the related notions of pupil involvement, contracting and self-monitoring. In many senses, a good IEP, as discussed in this chapter, can become an expression of such a contract in a school setting.

The idea of direct payments may be less familiar to staff in schools and colleges. However, this way of devolving funding directly to service users, so that they can define and purchase their own services, is becoming more common in work with adults with learning disabilities, including those with profound and complex learning disabilities (see, for example, Holman and Collins 1998). It may be that staff working with students in schools and colleges will wish to develop systems whereby students begin to regard themselves as 'consumers' of aspects of their education, with the right to choose the courses they prefer to attend. It is certainly true that staff need to begin to prepare their students for the experience of managing direct payments in their adult lives.

With regard to the independence of the person-centred planning process, we certainly do not wish to encourage professionals to adopt this approach wholesale as an alternative to existing planning procedures. It is important that person-centred planning operates in neutral territory. To professionalise it and to bring it under the control of one or another of the statutory services would be to destroy one of its major advantages for people with learning difficulties and their families. We also suggest that procedures for planning meetings held under the jurisdiction of the statutory agencies have formal functions which lie outside the remit of person-centred planning. We do suggest, however, that professionals need to take account of the principles and practices associated with person-centred planning. They may wish to do this in a number of ways, for example:

- staff may encourage people with learning difficulties, their families and their enablers and supporters to bring the outcomes of their own person-centred planning processes into school or college in order to make them part of an annual review or a parents' evening;
- staff may be invited to participate in person-centred planning procedures which are initiated and controlled by people with learning difficulties, their families and their enablers and supporters;
- staff may wish to use some of the features of person-centred planning which we have set out here in order to promote pupils' and students' involvement in planning procedures undertaken in school or college.

We suggest that each of these possibilities will be likely to enhance pupils' and students' personal and social development in obvious ways.

Promoting the involvement of pupils and students

We have emphasised many times in this chapter that pupils and students should be fully involved in the processes of negotiating targets for learning and reviewing their progress. The person-centred planning procedures described above have involvement as a core principle. Some of the examples of practices we have given in this chapter, and elsewhere in this book, offer insights into the processes of pupil and student involvement. In closing this chapter, and the book, we offer, as Figure 6.7, a staff development activity focused on clarifying ways of gathering the views and perceptions of pupils and students and bringing them into the teaching and learning arena. This activity is based on ideas in Lawson (1998) and, in presenting this material here, we acknowledge a debt to her work.

The instructions and the list of 'most useful factors' can be copied onto paper for distribution to participants. The sheets, divided into 10 boxes, most of them containing statements, should be copied onto card and cut up along the lines provided, making one set of cards for each group of four or five participants. We suggest you give each group of participants a set of cards and the instructions sheet. You should set aside about 30 minutes for the card-sorting activity. When each group of participants has an agreed set of 10 statements, hand out the 'most useful factors' sheet, which is simply a list of all the statements on the cards. As each group reports on their 10 selected statements, and any new statements they have written themselves, participants can make individual notes against this list. Allow time for further debate, sharing of views and suggestions for refinements in policy or practice in this plenary phase of the activity. We hope that the debates engendered among staff groups working through this activity help to promote more meaningful involvement for learners in a range of settings.

A summary of issues in the IEP process

This chapter contends that planning focused on individual priorities can promote pupils' and students' personal and social development in a range of ways. In order to be effective in this area, IEPs should:

- record those interventions put in place through Early Years Action, Early Years Action Plus or School Action and School Action Plus and for pupils with statements of special educational need;
- address priority areas of learning specific to an individual pupil experiencing difficulties;
- focus on a small number of targets for learning, probably drawn from key areas such as communication, literacy, numeracy, behaviour and personal and social skills;
- detail targets for learning which are additional to or different from those for most pupils;
- be subject to regular processes of monitoring and review which involve the pupil and help them to monitor their own progress.

In this sense, the process of developing, implementing and reviewing the IEP can in itself help to promote personal and social development, whatever the focus for the targets. In order to make this complementary relationship more effective, we would make a further series of suggestions:

- In terms of style, IEPs should be open and accessible to pupils, promoting their active involvement.
- In terms of form, IEPs should present and record information in ways which are accessible and available to pupils.

- The process of developing, implementing and reviewing IEPs should involve pupils meaningfully and in practice at all stages.
- The content of IEPs should focus on key issues in pupils' personal and social development, including key skills for learning and for adult life beyond school. The relevance of IEPs to pupils' priority needs, as well as their effectiveness, will be enhanced if pupils are encouraged to set targets for themselves.
- The outcome of an effective IEP will be a young person who is better prepared for life in an increasingly inclusive society, not necessarily someone who conforms to the narrow demands of school life. Pupils can be effectively involved in judging their own success against performance criteria which they have helped to establish for themselves.

Closing comments

In closing this book, we would like to make clear that we greet the acknowledgement of personal and social development in the National Curriculum with real enthusiasm. The handbooks for the National Curriculum (DfEE/QCA 1999a) and the guidelines for teaching pupils with learning difficulties (QCA/DfEE 2001abc) reveal that the whole curriculum is shot through with personal and social development – in the ethos of the school, in taught courses, in statements of values, in the implementation of the key skills – as the chapters of this book have demonstrated.

In some ways, staff who work with pupils with learning difficulties will regard this as representing a welcome return to previous curricular priorities. Many of the teaching programmes developed in specialist contexts in the past were constructed around a variety of interpretations of personal and social education. We accept that staff will find much that is familiar in the national guidance.

At the same time, we note that there are significant new challenges. We have tried to engage with many of these in this book, including issues in the development of education for work, for advocacy and for sexuality for people with learning difficulties. These issues, and other issues that will come to the fore as society and the expectations and demands of people with learning difficulties change, will continue to challenge us in the years to come. We suggest that the curriculum for personal and social development that ceases to challenge both practitioners and learners will fail to do justice to the constantly evolving adult realities faced by young people with learning difficulties in a changing world.

This activity requires you to work in groups of four or five in order to identify the 10 most important factors which, in your experience or opinion, enable staff to take account of pupils' and students' views.

Deal out the cards, in random order, to members of the group. Look at your cards and take turns in selecting the statement which you see as most significant in enabling staff to take account of pupils' and students' views. As you place this card on the table, tell the group why you consider this factor to be so important. Offer your colleagues an example, drawn from your own experience, of the good practice that can be developed through this way of working. Give a detailed description and encourage other participants to compare your example with their own experiences. Encourage cross-questioning and debate.

When 10 cards have been placed on the table, you should continue to read out, discuss and debate the inclusion of the statements on your remaining cards. You may wish to 'argue out' some of the cards already placed in order to include new ideas. As a group, you may develop your own means of negotiation to include or exclude statements or to formulate new statements which may be written on the blank cards provided. Your group should, however, work towards a final set of 10 agreed statements.

If there is time, you may wish to put your 10 statements in order of importance.

In the plenary stage of this activity, you will report back your negotiated statements and have a chance to compare, and debate, your own responses with those of other groups.

Figure 6.7a Taking account of pupils' views

A: use of signs and symbols

B: timetabled records of achievement sessions

C: use of photographs and video

D: tape recorded interviews

E: setting up tutor groups

F: staff training in counselling techniques

G: negotiating a whole school pastoral policy

H: setting personal and social education priorities for all pupils

I: offering opportunities for choices and decision making

J: consulting pupils during the annual review process

K: using advocates from outside school

L: following the Code of Practice

M: implementing the National Curriculum

N: setting up a pupil/student council

O: collating portfolios of samples of work

P: pupil goal setting

Q: teaching self advocacy skills

R: offering timetable options

S: working to OFSTED criteria

T: pupil self evaluation

U: including pupil contributions in reports

V: regular 1:1 sessions with pupils

W: use of information technology

X: encouraging interaction and group discussion

Y: making timetables and records accessible to pupils

Z: changing teaching styles

Figure 6.7b Most useful factors in taking account of pupil views . . .

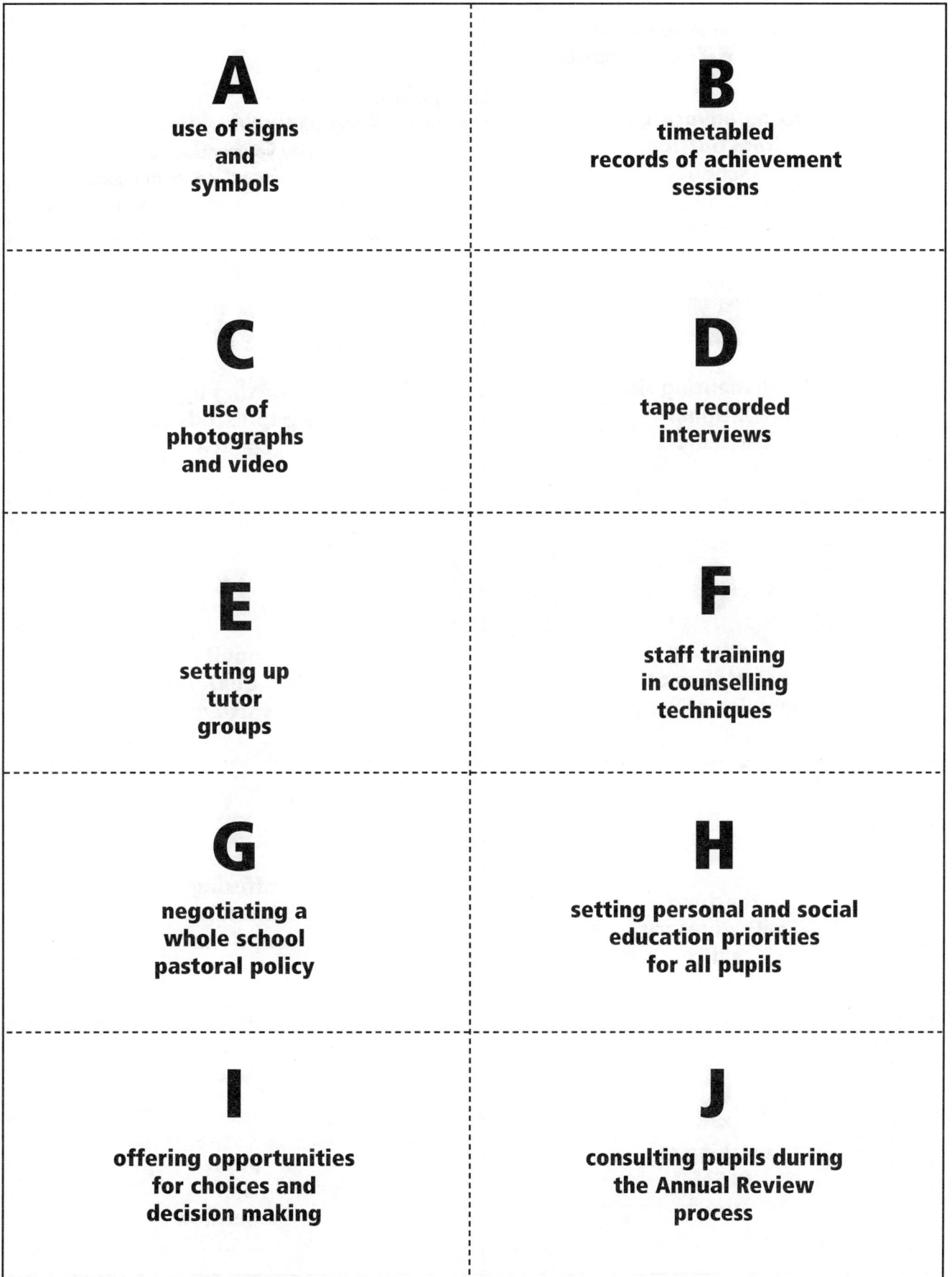

A
use of signs
and
symbols

B
timetabled
records of achievement
sessions

C
use of
photographs
and video

D
tape recorded
interviews

E
setting up
tutor
groups

F
staff training
in counselling
techniques

G
negotiating a
whole school
pastoral policy

H
setting personal and social
education priorities
for all pupils

I
offering opportunities
for choices and
decision making

J
consulting pupils during
the Annual Review
process

Figure 6.7c Cards for pupils views

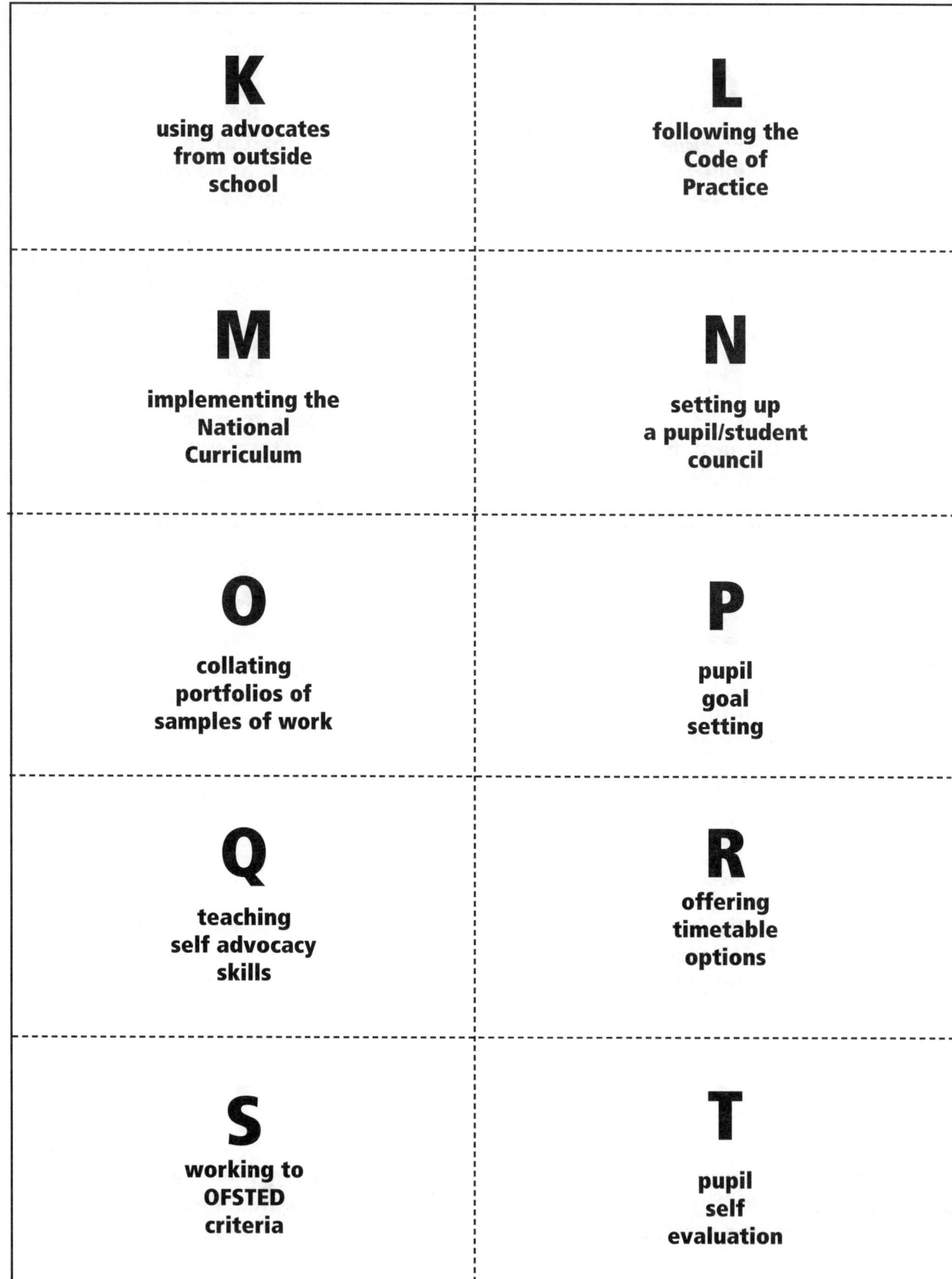

K
using advocates
from outside
school

L
following the
Code of
Practice

M
implementing the
National
Curriculum

N
setting up
a pupil/student
council

O
collating
portfolios of
samples of work

P
pupil
goal
setting

Q
teaching
self advocacy
skills

R
offering
timetable
options

S
working to
OFSTED
criteria

T
pupil
self
evaluation

Figure 6.7c (Continued)

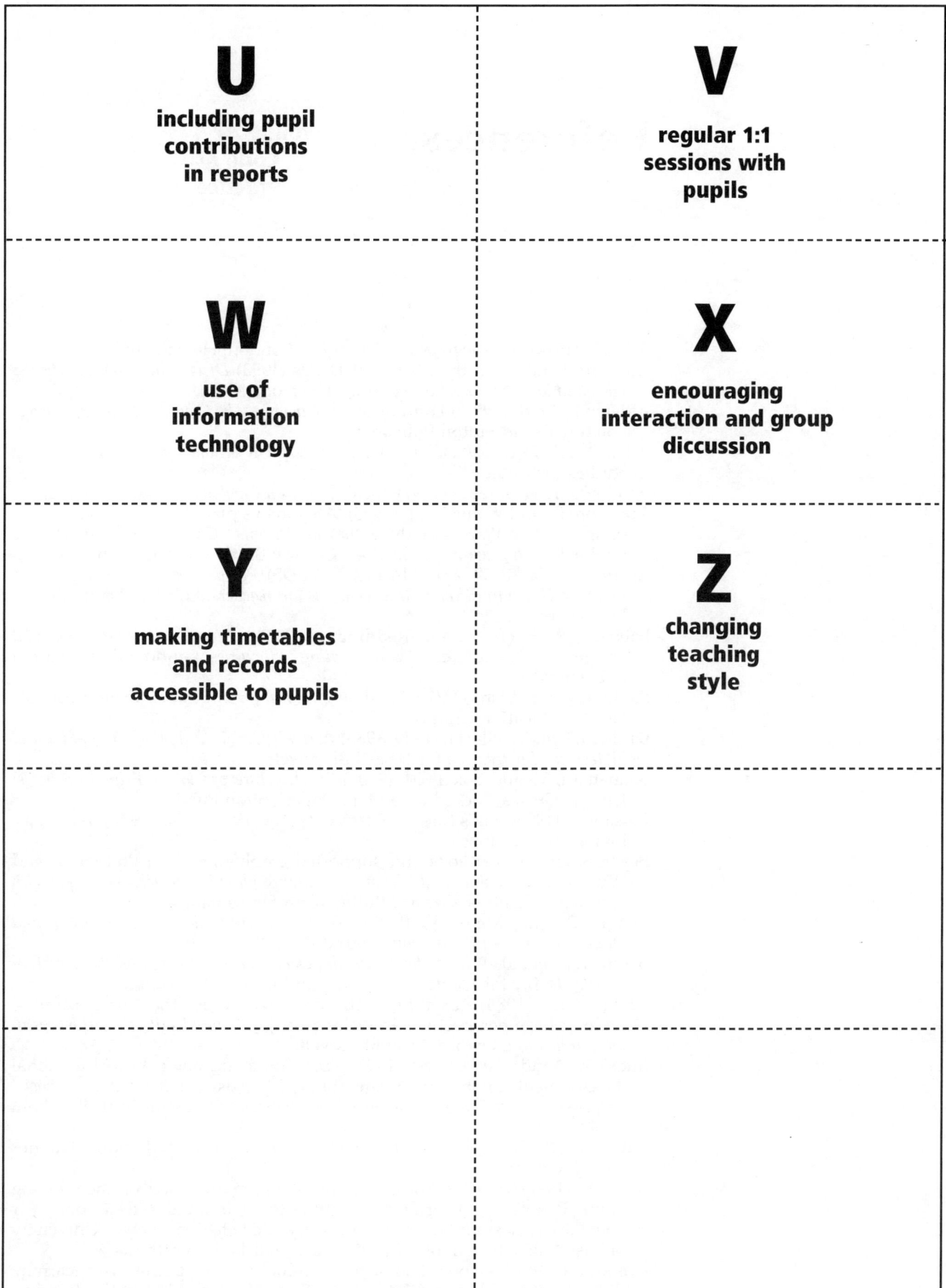

Figure 6.7c (Continued)

References

Abbs, P. (1974) *Autobiography in Education*. London: Heinemann.

Advisory Council on the Misuse of Drugs (1993) *Drug Education in Schools: The Need for New Impetus*. London: The Home Office.

Alderson, P. (ed.) (1999) *Learning and Inclusion – The Cleves School Experience*. London: David Fulton Publishers.

Allen, I. (1987) *Education in Sex and Personal Relationships*. London: Policy Studies Institute.

Ashdown, R. *et al.* (eds) (1991) *The Curriculum Challenge*. London: Falmer.

Atkinson, D. and Walmsley, J. (1995) 'A woman's place? Issues of gender', in Philpot, T. and Ward, L. (eds) *Values and Visions – Changing Ideas in Services for People with Learning Difficulties*. Oxford: Butterworth-Heinemann.

Ayers, H., Clarke, D. and Murray, A. (1995) *Perspectives on Behaviour – A Practical Guide to Effective Interventions for Teachers*. London: David Fulton Publishers.

Babbage, R., Byers, R. and Redding, H. (1999) *Approaches to Teaching and Learning: Including Pupils With Learning Difficulties*. London: David Fulton Publishers.

Balding, J. and Bish, D. (1992) *Alcohol Education in Schools*. Exeter: Schools Health Education Unit.

Baldwin, J. and Wells, H. (1979–1983) *Active Tutorial Work, Books One-Five and Sixteen to Nineteen*. Oxford: Basil Blackwell.

Bennathan, M. and Boxall, M. (2000) *Effective Intervention in Primary Schools: Nurture Groups*, 2nd edn. London: David Fulton Publishers.

Bessant, P. (1996) 'Pat's Life', in Bessant, P. *et al.*, *Positive Tales*. Milton Keynes: Living Archive Press.

Beyer, S. (1995) 'Real jobs and supported employment', in Philpot, T. and Ward, L. (eds) *Values and Visions – Changing Ideas in Services for People with Learning Difficulties*. Oxford: Butterworth-Heinemann.

Bolam, R. and Medlock, P. (1985) *Active Tutorial Work: Training and Dissemination: An Evaluation*. Oxford: Basil Blackwell.

Booth, T. *et al.* (2000) *Index for Inclusion: Developing Learning and Participation in Schools*. Bristol: Centre for Studies on Inclusive Education.

Bridges, D. (1986) 'Dealing with controversy in the curriculum: a philosophical perspective', in Wellington, J. J. (1986) *Controversial Issues in the Curriculum*. Oxford: Basil Blackwell.

Buck, M. and Inman, S. (1995) 'Setting a framework for personal development', in Inman, S. and Buck, M. (eds) *Adding Value? Schools' Responsibility for Personal and Social Development*. Stoke-on-Trent: Trentham Books.

Button, L. (1974) *Developmental Group Work with Adolescents*. London: Hodder and Stoughton.

Byers, R. (1997) 'Hearing Voices: An Investigation into Ways of Encouraging Young People with Learning Difficulties to Review and Reflect upon their own Experiences and to Formulate and Articulate their Views'. University of East Anglia School of Education: Unpublished MEd thesis.

Byers, R. (1998) 'Personal and social development for pupils with learning difficulties', in Tilstone, C. *et al.* (eds) *Promoting Inclusive Practice*. London: Routledge.

Byers, R. and Rose, R. (1996) *Planning the Curriculum for Pupils with Special Educational Needs – A Practical Guide*. London: David Fulton Publishers.

Caviglioli, O. (1997) 'Making it work', *Special Children*. October 1997: 15–19.

Clark, C. *et al.* (1997) *New Directions in Special Needs – Innovations in Mainstream Schools*. London: Cassell.

Claxton, G. (1999) *Wise Up: The Challenge of Lifelong Learning*. London: Bloomsbury.

Collis, M. and Lacey, P. (1996) *Interactive Approaches to Teaching – A Framework for INSET*. London: David Fulton Publishers.

Coupe O'Kane, J. and Goldbart, J. (1998) *Communication Before Speech – Development and Assessment*, 2nd edn. London: David Fulton Publishers.

Cowie, H. and Sharp, S. (1996) *Peer Counselling in Schools: A Time to Listen*. London: David Fulton Publishers.

Department of Health (1989) *The Children Act 1989*. London: HMSO.

DES (Department of Education and Science) (1989) *Planning for School Development*. London: HMSO.

Detheridge, T. and Detheridge, M. (1997) *Literacy Through Symbols – Improving Access for Children and Adults*. London: David Fulton Publishers.

DFE (Department for Education) (1994) *Code of Practice on the Identification and Assessment of Special Educational Needs*. London: HMSO.

DfEE (Department for Education and Employment) (1998) *Excellence for All: Meeting Special Educational Needs: A Programme of Action*. London: DfEE.

DfEE (1999a) *National Healthy School Standard: Getting Started*. Nottingham: DfEE.

DfEE (1999b) *Preparing Young People for Adult Life*. A report by the National Advisory Group on Personal, Social and Health Education. Nottingham: DfEE publications.

DfEE (1999c) *Special Educational Needs: Consultation Document on the Proposed Revision of the Code of Practice*. London: DfEE.

DfEE (2000a) *Sex and Relationship Education Guidance*. Circular 0016. London: DfEE.

DfEE (2000b) *SEN Code of Practice on the Identification and Assessment of Pupils with Special Educational Needs – Draft for Consultation*. London: DfEE.

DfEE (2000c) *ConneXions – The ConneXions Service – Prospectus and Specifications*. Nottingham: DfEE.

DfEE/QCA (Department for Education and Employment and Qualifications and Curriculum Authority) (1999a) *The National Curriculum – Handbook for Teachers in England*. London: DfEE/QCA.

DfEE/QCA (1999b) *The National Curriculum for England: Non-statutory Frameworks for Personal, Social and Health Education and Citizenship at Key Stages 1 & 2; Personal, Social and Health Education at Key Stages 3 & 4*. London: HMSO.

Downs, C. and Craft, A. (1997a) *Sex in Context – Safeguards in Systems: A Handbook*. Brighton: Pavilion Publishing.

Downs, C. and Craft, A. (1997b) *Sex in Context – A Personal and Social Development Programme for Children and Adults with Profound and Multiple Impairments: Parts One and Two*. Brighton: Pavilion Publishing.

Dunn, J. (1993) *Young Children's Close Relationships: Beyond Attachment*. London: Sage.

Faulkner, D. *et al.* (eds) (1998) *Learning Relationships in the Classroom*. London and New York: Routledge/Open University.

FEFC (Further Education Funding Council) (1996) *Inclusive Learning – Principles and Recommendations* (summary of the Tomlinson report). Coventry: FEFC.

Fergusson, A. (1994) 'Planning for communication', in Rose, R. *et al.* (eds) *Implementing the Whole Curriculum for Pupils with Learning Difficulties*. London: David Fulton Publishers.

Florian, L. (1998) 'Inclusive practice: what, why and how?', in Tilstone, C. *et al.* (eds) *Promoting Inclusive Practice*. London: Routledge.

Ford, K. *et al.* (1998) *An Analysis of Research into the Impact of the National Curriculum and the Implications for Teachers and Schools*. Newcastle-upon-Tyne: University of Newcastle/ QCA.

Gardner, H. (1993) *Frames of Mind: The Theory of Multiple Intelligences*, 2nd edn. Glasgow: Fontana.

Goleman, D. (1996) *Emotional Intelligence*. London: Bloomsbury.

Griffiths, M. (1994) *Transition to Adulthood – The Role of Education for Young People with Severe Learning Difficulties.* London: David Fulton Publishers.

Gysbers, N. (1990) *Comprehensive Guidance Programs that Work.* Michigan: ERIC.

Hall, J. (1996) 'Integration, inclusion – what does it all mean?', in Coupe O'Kane, J. and Goldbart, J. (eds) *Whose Choice? – Contentious Issues for Those Working with People with Learning Difficulties.* London: David Fulton Publishers.

Hamblin, D. (1978) *The Teacher and Pastoral Care.* Oxford: Basil Blackwell.

Hart, S. (1996) *Beyond Special Needs – Enhancing Children's Learning through Innovative Thinking.* London: Paul Chapman Publishing.

Haste, H. (1999) 'Moral understanding in socio-cultural context – lay social theory and Vygotskian synthesis', in Woodhead, M. *et al.* (1999) *Making Sense of Moral Development.* London: Routledge/Open University.

HMI (Her Majesty's Inspectorate of Schools) (1979) *Aspects of Secondary Education in England.* London: HMSO.

Holman, A. and Collins, J. (1998) 'Choice and control: making direct payments work for people with learning difficulties', in Ward, L. (ed.) *Innovations in Advocacy and Empowerment for People with Intellectual Disabilities.* Chorley, Lancs: Lisieux Hall.

Hopson, B. and Scally, M. (1981) *Lifeskills Teaching.* Maidenhead: McGraw Hill.

Hutton, W. (1995) *The State We're In.* London: Jonathan Cape.

Jelly, M. *et al.* (2000) *Involving Pupils in Practice – Promoting Partnerships with Pupils with Special Educational Needs.* London: David Fulton Publishers.

Johns, R. *et al.* (1997) *Let's do It! Creative Activities for Sex Education for Young People with Learning Difficulties.* London: Image in Action.

Jones, K and Charlton, T. (1996) *Overcoming Learning and Behaviour Difficulties: Partnerships with Pupils.* London: Routledge.

Kolb, D. (1984) *Experiential Learning: Experience as the Source of Learning and Development.* Englewood Cliffs, NJ: Prentice-Hall.

Lawson, H. (1998) *Practical Record Keeping – Development and Resource Material for Staff Worjking with Pupils with Special Educational Needs,* 2nd edn. London: David Fulton Publishers.

McBrien, J. and Foxen, T. (1981) *Training Staff in Behavioural Methods: The EDY In-Service Course for Mental Handicap Practitioners.* Manchester: Manchester University Press.

McLaughlin, C. (2000) 'The emotional challenge of listening and dialogue', *Pastoral Care in Education* **18** (3), 16–21.

McLaughlin, C. *et al.* (1996) *Counselling and Guidance in Schools: Developing Policy and Practice.* London: David Fulton Publishers.

Mental Health Foundation (1999) *The Big Picture.* London: the Mental Health Foundation.

Mittler, P. (1996) 'Preparing for self-advocacy', in Carpenter, B. *et al.* (eds) *Enabling Access – Effective Teaching and Learning for Pupils with Learning Difficulties.* London: David Fulton Publishers.

Mosley, J. (1996) *Quality Circle Time in the Primary Classroom.* Wisbech: Learning Development Aids.

NCB (National Children's Bureau) (2001) *A Charter for Good Sex and Relationships Education.* www.ncb.org.uk/sexed.htm

NCC (National Curriculum Council) (1989) *The National Curriculum and Whole Curriculum Planning,* Circular no 6. York: National Curriculum Council.

NCC (1990a) *The Whole Curriculum.* Curriculum Guidance 3. York: National Curriculum Council.

NCC (1990b) *Curriculum Guidance and Education for Citizenship.* York: National Curriculum Council.

Nind, M. and Hewett, D. (1994) *Access to Communication – Developing the Basics of Communication with People with Severe Learning Difficulties through Intensive Interaction.* London: David Fulton Publishers.

Nind, M. and Hewett, D. (1998) 'Commentary three: learners with autism', in Hewett, D. and Nind, M. (eds) *Interaction in Action – Reflections on the Use of Intensive Interaction.* London: David Fulton Publishers.

OECD/CERI (1986) *Young People with Handicaps: The Road to Adulthood*. Paris: OECD.

OFSTED (Office for Standards in Education) (1998) *The Annual Report of Her Majesty's Chief Inspector of Schools: Standards and Quality in Education 1996–1997*. London: The Stationery Office.

OFSTED (1999) *Handbook for Inspecting Special Schools and Pupil Referral Units – With Guidance on Self-evaluation*. London: The Stationery Office.

OFSTED (2000) *Drug Education in Schools: An Update. Sept. 2000*. London: OFSTED.

OFSTED (2001) *Evaluating Educational Inclusion*. London: OFSTED Available online at http://www.ofsted.gov.uk

Otten, L. (ed.) (1999) *A Curriculum for Personal and Social Education*. London: David Fulton Publishers.

Perkins, D. (1995) *Outsmarting IQ; The Emerging Science of Learnable Intelligence*. New York: The Free Press.

Pring, R. (1984) *Personal and Social Education in the Curriculum*. Sevenoaks: Hodder and Stoughton.

Project Inclusion for Newham Council (1997) *Inclusive Education Audit*. London: Newham Council Education Office.

QCA (Qualifications and Curriculum Authority) (1998) *Education for Citizenship and the Teaching of Democracy in Schools*. The Crick Report. London: QCA.

QCA (2000) *Personal and Social Education and Citizenship at Key Stages 3and 4 (and 1 and 2); Initial Guidance for Schools*. London: QCA.

QCA/DfEE (2001a) *Planning, Teaching and Assessing the Curriculum for Pupils with Learning Difficulties – General Guidelines*. London: QCA/DfEE.

QCA/DfEE (2001b) *Planning, Teaching and Assessing the Curriculum for Pupils with Learning Difficulties – Developing Skills*. London: QCA/DfEE.

QCA/DfEE (2001c) *Planning, Teaching and Assessing the Curriculum for Pupils with Learning Difficulties – Personal, Social and Health Education and Citizenship*. London: QCA/DfEE.

QCA/DfEE (2001d) *Personal, Social and Health Education and Citizenship*. London: QCA.

Ramjhun, A. F. (1995) *Implementing the Code of Practice for Children with Special Educational Needs – A Practical Guide*. London: David Fulton Publishers.

Reynolds, B. and Caviglioli, O. (1999) 'Aiming true', *Special Children* January 1999, 25–8.

Rogers, B. (1991) *You Know the Fair Rule: Strategies for Making the Hard Job of Discipline in Schools Easier*. Harlow: Longman.

Rose, R. (1991) 'A jigsaw approach to group work', *British Journal of Special Education* **18** (2), 54–7.

Rudduck, J. *et al.* (1996) *School Improvement – What Pupils Can Tell Us*. London: David Fulton Publishers.

Rushton, P. and Harwick, J. (1994) 'Pupil participation in their own Records of Achievement', in Rose, R. *et al.* (eds) *Implementing the Whole Curriculum for Pupils with Learning Difficulties*. London: David Fulton Publishers.

Rutter, M. (1991) 'Pathways to Adult Life', *Pastoral Care in Education* **6** (2) 3–10.

Ryder, J. and Campbell, L. (1988) *Balancing Acts in Personal and Social Education*. London: Routledge.

Sanderson, H. (1998) 'A say in my future: involving people with profound and multiple disabilities in person centred planning', in Ward, L. (ed.) *Innovations in Advocacy and Empowerment for People with Intellectual Disabilities*. Chorley, Lancs: Lisieux Hall.

SCAA (School Curriculum and Assessment Authority) (1995) *Planning the Curriculum at Key Stages 1 and 2*. London: SCAA.

SCAA (School Curriculum and Assessment Authority) (1996) *Planning the Curriculum for Pupils with Profound and Multiple Learning Difficulties*. London: SCAA.

Scott-Bauman, A. (1996) 'Listen to the child', in Jones, K. and Charlton, T. (eds) *Overcoming Learning and Behaviour Difficulties – Partnership with Pupils*. London: Routledge.

SEAC (School Examination and Assessment Council) (1990) *Records of Achievement in Primary Schools*. London: SEAC.

Sebba, J. (1995) *Geography for All*. London: David Fulton Publishers.

Sebba, J. and Ainscow, M. (1996) 'International developments in inclusive schooling: mapping the issues', *Cambridge Journal of Education* **26** (1), 5–18.

Sebba, J. and Sachdev, D. (1997) *What Works in Inclusive Education?* Ilford, Essex: Barnardo's.

Sebba, J. *et al.* (1993) *Redefining the Whole Curriculum for Pupils with Learning Difficulties.* London: David Fulton Publishers.

Skrtic, T. M. (1991) 'Students with special educational needs: artefacts of the traditional curriculum', in Ainscow, M. (ed.) *Effective Schools for All.* London: David Fulton Publishers.

Slavin, R. E. (1990) *Co-operative Learning: Theory, Research and Practice.* Englewood Cliffs, NJ: Prentice-Hall.

Stanford, G. and Stoate, P. (1990) *Developing Effective Classroom Groups: A Practical Guide for Teachers.* Bishop Sutton, Bristol: Acora Books.

Tilstone, C. (1991) 'Pupils' views', in Tilstone, C. (ed.) *Teaching Pupils with Severe Learning Difficulties.* London: David Fulton Publishers.

Tilstone, C. *et al.* (2000) *Pupils with Learning Difficulties in Mainstream Schools.* London: David Fulton Publishers.

Tisdall, E. K. M. (1994) 'Why not consider citizenship?: a critique of post-school transitional models for young disabled people', *Disability and Society* **9** (1), 3–17.

TTA (Teacher Training Agency) (1999) *National Special Educational Needs Specialist Standards.* London: TTA.

Tuckman, B.W. (1965) 'Developmental Sequence in Small Groups', *Psychological Bulletin* **63,** 384–99.

Tyne, J. (1994) 'Advocacy: not just another subject', in Rose, R. *et al.* (eds) *Implementing the Whole Curriculum for Pupils with Learning Difficulties.* London: David Fulton Publishers.

UNESCO (United Nations Educational, Scientific and Cultural Organisation) (1994) *The Salamanca Statement and Framework for Action on Special Educational Needs.* Paris: UNESCO.

Wall, W. D. (1977) *Constructive Education for Adolescents.* London: Harrap/UNESCO.

Ware, J. (1996) *Creating a Responsive Environment – For People with Profound and Multiple Learning Difficulties.* London: David Fulton Publishers.

Watkins, C. (1995) 'Personal-social education and the whole curriculum', in Best, R. *et al.* (eds) (1995) *Pastoral Care and Personal-social Education: Entitlement and Provision.* London: Cassell.

Watkins, C. (1999) 'Personal-social Education: Beyond the National Curriculum', *British Journal of Guidance and Counselling* **27** (1), 71–84.

Weare, K. (2000) *Promoting Mental, Emotional and Social Health.* London: Routledge.

Winup, K. (1994) 'The role of a student committee in the promotion of independence among school leavers', in Coupe O' Kane, J. and Smith, B. (eds) *Taking Control: Enabling People with Learning Difficulties.* London: David Fulton Publishers.

WHO (World Health Organisation) (1998) *WHO's Global School Health Initiative; Health Promoting Schools.*

Zarkowska, E. and Clements, J. (1994) *Problem Behaviour and People with Severe Learning Difficulties – the STAR Approach*, 2nd edn. London: Chapman and Hall.

Useful websites and addresses

OFSTED	www.ofsted.gov.uk
Sex Education Forum	www.ncb.org.uk/sexed.htm
Qualifications and Curriculum Authority	www.qca.org.uk
National Curriculum inclusion website	www.nc.uk.net

Image in Action – Chinnor Road, Bledlow Ridge, High Wycombe, Bucks. HP14 4AJ

Index